W9-BBK-581

322
C66c

84030

DATE DUE			
Nov 26 '73			
May 5 '75			
Dec 14 7 9			
Jul 6 '83			

WITHDRAWN

CIVIL DISOBEDIENCE

CIVIL DISOBEDIENCE

CONSCIENCE, TACTICS, AND THE LAW

Carl Cohen

1971
COLUMBIA UNIVERSITY PRESS
NEW YORK AND LONDON

CARL A. RUDISILL LIBRARY
LENOIR RHYNE COLLEGE

Carl Cohen is Associate Professor of Philosophy at The University of Michigan and Associate Director of The Residential College at The University of Michigan.

322
C66c
84030
July 1973

Copyright © 1971 Columbia University Press
ISBN: 0-231-08646-6

Printed in the United States of America

9 8 7 6 5 4 3

TO MURIEL

FOREWORD

Some of the central ideas of this book were first presented, in much abbreviated form, in the pages of *The Nation*, whose editors have graciously supported and warmly encouraged their later development. I acknowledge here my debt to them, first; second, to the Captain and crew of the M/S *Roseville*, of the Barber Line, whose sparkling decks so long served as my study; and third, to my students at The University of Michigan, whose idealism and intelligence have helped both to inspire my work and to improve it.

Many will not find what I say about civil disobedience entirely palatable at first. I beg the reader to pursue the argument to its end before appraising it; and whatever his final judgment of civil disobedience or its practitioners, I take the liberty of reminding him that many of the causes for the sake of which civil disobedience has been courageously undertaken remain our pressing moral concerns. "The great interests of humanity" William Ellery Channing said, having the abolitionists in mind, "do not lose their claims on us because sometimes injudiciously maintained."

CONTENTS

CIVIL DISOBEDIENCE

WHAT CIVIL DISOBEDIENCE IS

1. DISOBEDIENCE AND RESPECT FOR LAW

The life of every civilized community is governed by rules. Neither peace of mind for the present nor intelligent planning for the future is possible for men who either live without rules or cannot abide by the rules they have. Making rules for the community, and enforcing them, is the job of government. No community can be truly civilized, therefore, without an effective and reasonably stable government. That is why the international community, whose rules are few, often broken, and badly enforced, is largely an uncivilized community, while within the many nation states may be found every degree of community order, from the chaotic to the over-organized. An established government, providing and maintaining an effective system of laws, is certainly not by itself a sufficient condition of happy human life, but it is, with few exceptions, a necessary condition of such life.

The maintenance of a stable system of laws supposes that the government, however constituted, has the power to perform its rule-making and rule-enforcing jobs. But sheer power in the hands of government is not enough. In the long run a system of laws can remain effective, and a community orderly, only when the members of that community respect the laws. Civilized human life requires, therefore, that at least the vast majority of citizens recognize the authority of some law-making body, and that they accept the laws enacted by that body as their own, properly governing them. In short, the civilized human being sees himself as a member of the *civitas*, the civic community, and accepts, as a duty flowing from that membership, the obligation to obey its laws.

Respect for the law being so central an element in the good life, any course of conduct that aims deliberately at disobedience of the law, and does so not merely for the sake of private gain but in the honest belief that such disobedience is essential for some greater social good, must be either the product of sheer stupidity or the paradoxical result of balancing conflicting obligations and goods, of which obedience to that law is only one. Some cases of deliberate disobedience of law are not the product of selfishness or of sheer stupidity. Honorable and intelligent men may knowingly violate certain laws of their community in what they reflectively conclude to be a larger interest. To understand such conduct deeply, or to pass judgment upon it fairly, one must undertake the same task of weighing moral and political factors as that undertaken by the violators themselves. Their civil disobedience is a political and/or a moral act. It may be undertaken on the crest of passion; but even more than most political and moral acts, it will require rational defense. Those who deliberately engage in civil disobedience are usually ready and anxious to present that defense. Its appraisal requires the probing of some deep and difficult issues, some of which perennially recur, and perennially elude definitive resolution.

Inquiry into the nature and possible justifications of civil disobedience is the object of this book. If respect for the law and obedience to it are basic social goods, under what circumstances can deliberate disobedience of that law be a greater good? The search for such circumstances—whether or not they are actually found—goes straight to the heart of the most fundamental questions of political philosophy: How sacred is the law of the state? Are there limits to the authority of state government over its citizens? If so, where are these limits? Who determines the violations of them? In what manner? How serious, and how clear, must be the injustice of the law before the citizen is justified in taking into his own hands the decision to break that law? Or is there no such degree of injustice? And if the laws themselves are just but the social or economic system they support is cruel and oppressive, might deliberate disobedience of the laws ever prove a justifiable instrument of political or moral protest?

2. PRELIMINARY OBJECTIVES

First among the issues to be dealt with is the *nature* of civil disobedience. Any effort to determine whether, how, and under what circumstances civil disobedience might be justified presupposes a reasonably clear understanding of what it is. This is a matter upon which substantial agreement can be reached. Political and philosophical categories cannot be delineated with mathematical precision, of course; we must expect that, however thorough the account, borderline cases will arise, and some questions of interpretation will remain unanswered. Still, through clarity of language and clarity of thought, we can identify the essential features of what is generally understood by the expression "civil disobedience." We can distinguish it from other forms of protest, and from other forms of law-breaking. We can explore the relations between civil disobedience and other distinct concepts sometimes confounded with it; and we can distinguish different kinds of civil disobedience, identifying the several problems that attend each kind.

These things can be accomplished. To remedy the looseness of common parlance we may be obliged at some points to adopt terminological conventions in some degree arbitrary. The whole may come to appear more exact than any philosophical inquiry can ever really be. But with careful analysis the essential preliminary objectives can be attained. We can construct an intellectual framework within which cases of civil disobedience, and the issues arising out of such cases, can be properly differentiated and clearly understood. In plain language, we can develop the tools with which the further critique of civil disobedience may be pursued.

3. DISOBEDIENCE

An act of civil disobedience is an act that breaks the law. However vehement, radical, or extraordinary is one's protest, if he does not break the law he has not been disobedient. The violation of some law of the body politic is a universal and necessary feature of the conduct that here concerns us. That violation may take the form of doing something the law forbids (e.g., disturbing the peace by continual shouting) or of refusing to do something the law commands (e.g., deliberately failing to register for the military draft). Whether in the form of a "positive" or a "negative" act, as these are sometimes called in the courts, an act of civil disobedience necessarily incorporates some infraction of the law.

This law-breaking character of civil disobedience is at once its most notable feature and the source of much of the puzzlement it creates. Taken by itself, law-breaking is wrong. It isn't merely culpable in some technical or legal sense, though it is that too; more deeply, it is wrong because (excluding for the present the possibility of a cruel and tyrannical government) every citizen has more than a legal obligation to obey the laws. His obligation to obey is a general and moral duty arising out of his role as citizen. And that duty is specially compelling in a democracy, where citizens participate, or have a right to participate, in making the laws of their community.

Of course many acts that, when taken by themselves, are wrongful may prove right and justifiable when considered in the light of their full circumstances. The context may present other moral considerations that clearly override the apparent wrongfulness of the act when described independent of that context. This is no more than plain common sense in many human affairs. To break a promise deliberately is wrong, though not usually a legal wrong. Yet there are times when it is morally essential that one break a promise he has given. My promise to meet a friend at a certain time and place is surely overridden if an emergency endangering the life of another requires my attention in a way that prevents me from keeping my appointment or even explaining my absence. Were my friend told only that I deliberately failed to appear, he might well be angry and bear a moral grievance against me, if only a minor one. When all the circumstances are later explained, he will surely agree, if he is reasonable and morally sensitive, that in view of the greater obligation to assist one in serious peril I am not only excused for failing to appear but was morally obliged to do as I did.

Nothing surprising here. Ethical theorists say that one has a prima facie obligation to keep his promises, but that one's ultimate or actual obligation in any complex situation will require the careful weighing of several, perhaps many prima facie obligations, some of which may conflict head on with others. We may think of such prima facie obligations as components, or vectors, pushing us in differing directions with differing degrees of force, the morally correct outcome of the set being our *resultant* obligation.

Every citizen of a lawful government, then, has a prima facie duty to obey its laws. That is true whatever the form of government, providing the authorities have been duly constituted and their laws and administration of them are reasonably just. Where each citizen has a proportionate voice in the making of policy and the framing of laws (either directly or through representatives), his acceptance of this role as partial legislator commits him yet more strongly to abide by the laws of that body. In a democracy, the prima facie obligation of obedience to the law has particular force; it is a component of considerable importance in determining the resultant obligations of democratic citizens.

Every civil disobedient faces the fact that his conduct, being disobedient, is prima facie wrong. The burden of showing that it is, nevertheless, his resultant obligation to disobey under those circumstances rests, necessarily, upon him. If his act is reflectively performed—as with most civil disobedients it is—he will be prepared to specify those other moral components in the situation that (as he argues) oblige him to do as he does. His undertaking is a serious one, because his obligation to obey the law is serious, and the considerations he hopes to show to be overriding must be weighty indeed. But it would be foolish and even irrational to suppose beforehand that he could never succeed in providing that defense. How he might proceed in doing so is a major topic for later discussion. (See Chapter V.)

One feature of the disobedient's violation of law is specially notable. He not only breaks the law but does so knowingly and deliberately. This is important. It means the disobedience itself is an essential, not an accidental, element in his act. In determining the justifiability of his conduct, this knowledge will have to be taken into account. When, for example, one who engages in a parade of protest unknowingly violates some municipal ordinance of which he was wholly unaware, we would not think him, for that reason, a civil disobedient; disobedience was not his specific intention. He too may be subject to punishment for his minor infraction—every man being presumed to know the law—but it is unlikely that legal action will be taken against such a person, and if it is, the fact that his infraction was committed unknowingly may properly serve as a mitigating factor in determining punishment. The civil disobedient, on the other hand, means to break the law. That is part—an essential part—of his intention. What role, if any, this should play in determining his appropriate legal punishment is a matter we shall take up later. (See Chapter IV, Section 2.) In any event, the deliberate and knowing character of his act is important for its full comprehension, and for its moral evaluation.

The civil disobedient breaks the law of the civic community; that is the chief reason his act receives the name it

Case 1. That acts of deliberate disobedience in the military, even when intended as instruments of protest or conscientious refusal, are likely to be met with severe punishment, may be illustrated by the following two examples.

(a) Three American soldiers, the "Fort Hood Three"—Pfc. James Johnson, Pvt. David Samas, and Pvt. Dennis Mora— announced in a press conference on 30 June 1966 that they would refuse to obey orders to fight in Vietnam. Their statement, reprinted in The Michigan Daily *(12 November 1966), read in part:*

We . . . have decided to take a stand against this war, which we consider immoral, illegal, and unjust. We have made our decision. We will not be a part of this unjust, immoral, and illegal war. We want no part of a war of extermination. We oppose the criminal waste of American lives and resources. We refuse to go to Vietnam.

In September of that year they were court-martialed for refusing to obey a direct order to board a plane that would have transported them to Vietnam, and they were convicted. In the course of the trial the law officer of the court said: "It is a matter of law that the war in Vietnam is legal, and I therefore forbid you to argue before this court that it isn't." Samas and Johnson were

does. Some acts of deliberate disobedience are like civil disobedience in every way, save that the code violated is not a civil code but some other—the regulations of some university, or trade union, or some military code. In the military context, where the penalties for disobedience are extremely severe, we may treat deliberate disobedience in basically the same way as we would were the code of civilian origin. (See Case 1.) In the case of deliberate disobedience of school, club, or other regulations not having the sanction of civil authority behind them, we are not dealing with civil disobedience in the strict sense. The punishment for disobedience of such rules can, *sentenced to five years imprisonment at hard labor in the Federal penitentiary at Fort Leavenworth, Kansas, and Mora to three years; all were to forfeit all pay and allowances and to receive dishonorable discharges from the U.S. Army. In accepting his sentence, Pvt. Mora said:*

I do not want to have to excuse my participation in the war in Vietnam in the only way that Adolph Eichmann would do, by explaining "the question of conscience is a matter for the head of state." On the contrary, I believe the matter of conscience is an individual responsibility.

(b) Michael Wittels, an artist and resident of Philadelphia, decided while in the Army Reserve that he could not kill and could no longer serve in the military. His experiences, related in The Saturday Evening Post *(Bill Davidson, "Hell, No, We Won't Go," January 1968), exhibit the penalties to which the military disobedient exposes himself. He applied for a conscientious-objector discharge, but was refused. When ordered to report to Fort Knox for forty-five days active duty he did so, but in civilian clothes, explaining that he could not wear the uniform and could not serve. After some delay he was given a direct order to put his uniform on and report for duty. Wittels respectfully refused and was taken to*

however, under some circumstances, be quite severe—expulsion from university, for example, or the loss of vital employment opportunities. Hence we may be justified in treating deliberate violations of these noncivic rules as marginal cases of civil disobedience, or as closely analogous to civil disobedience. Because in these cases the code violated has not the force of the whole civil community behind it, the duty to obey (which is deliberately unfulfilled) is not as weighty. Still, there is that prima facie duty, and in these marginal cases as well as in clear cases the disobedient will face the task of justifying his deliberate disobedience.

the stockade, where a sergeant told him, "We've had your kind in here before, and we're going to break you." His shirt, shoes, and socks were stripped off, and he was locked in an isolation cell, 6 feet by 8 feet, called "the Box"; it contained only a Bible and a steel slab for a bunk. He was forced to remain standing until 2:00 A.M., when he was sent to take a shower. Upon return to his cell his blanket was gone. It was a cold night; a guard said, "You don't want that blanket. It says U.S. Army on it." He was kept in "the Box" for three days and was fed bread, dry cereal, and cabbage. Two weeks later he was court-martialed for refusing to obey the direct order to put on his uniform, was convicted, and was sentenced to six months at hard labor. Upon completion of his sentence he was released from the stockade and returned to his Fort Knox unit where again he was ordered to put on his uniform and report for duty. Again he refused, and he was returned to the stockade. This time Wittels faced a general court-martial and a possible sentence of five years imprisonment at Fort Leavenworth. He was made a maximum custody prisoner, handcuffed, and put under armed guard. Finally, as a result of pressure from his Congressman, to whom his mother had appealed, Wittels was released and sent home. In July 1967, he received a general discharge, under honorable conditions, by reason of conscientious objection. ৡ

Strictly speaking, however, civil disobedience entails the violation of the civil code, the law of the political community—town, state, or country—of which the disobedient is himself a member.

4. DISOBEDIENCE AS PROTEST

Not every act that deliberately breaks the law is an act of civil disobedience. He who robs a bank, or beats his neighbor in anger, or drives his automobile recklessly, may commit any one of these or similar acts with full knowledge that such conduct is outlawed. Mere knowledge of the unlawfulness does not make it civil disobedience. Most criminal conduct is deliberate in that sense and is undertaken by its perpetrators either in the belief that they will not be caught, or in a state of mind (possibly induced by intoxicants, or passion, or mental disorder) in which the actor simply does not think or care about the outcome, though he knows his act is legally wrong. Interest in civil disobedience, therefore, centers around a class of unlawful acts rather narrowly restricted by the requirement that such acts manifest other essential features concurrently. The civil disobedient must do more than knowingly break the law.

Absolutely essential is the further element of *protest*. While this is an easy notion to grasp in a general way, it is not easy to specify what features of an act show it to be an act of protest. It is at least clear that an act of protest is not an act undertaken for the sake of private gain. Most protests are registered at the expense of considerable effort and inconvenience on the part of the protesters. They may hope for some ultimate personal advantage, but such advantage is not the primary motivation of their act. In the case of civil disobedient protests, the inconvenience to the protester is likely to be great, at a minimum; in most cases he is likely to suffer pains going far beyond inconvenience—in the form of legal punishments, financial losses, and personal humiliations, and very possibly all three. That the civil disobedient pursues his chosen course with the virtual certainty of some of these penalties ensuing provides some assurance that his act is, indeed, a form of protest.

Mere personal suffering is not itself fundamental, however, for there are always those who, foreseeing such consequences, persist in illegal acts out of an unbalanced desire for sheer notoriety, or self-mortification. Beyond the pains incurred is the cause for which they are suffered. Every genuine act of civil disobedience has such a cause, some larger goal or principle for whose sake the disobedient consciously breaks the law, sacrificing himself.

The act of sacrifice is a form of protest, because the civil disobedient invariably takes himself to be acting *against* some form of injustice that he finds intolerable. Such conduct is motivated not merely by the desire to achieve some social good but by the intense wish to eliminate some serious social evil. The protester seeks to act effectively against some element in his society that he cannot (as he believes) combat with hope of success by using less extreme devices. So we rightly say that all civil disobedience is a form of protest. It is a cry of conscience, publicized and concretized in the act of disobedience.

Protest, of course, may be wise or foolish, appropriate or inappropriate. In saying that the civil disobedient gives, in his act, a public demonstration of his moral convictions, we say nothing about the rightness or wisdom of those convictions. Civil disobedience may be practiced by crackpots, although in fact it is far more commonly practiced by persons who are reflective, unselfish, and deeply committed. Determining whether civil disobedience is wise or appropriate, however, is an important concern quite separable from the immediate one of understanding what it is.

5. PROTEST: LAWFUL AND UNLAWFUL

It should not need to be said that most social protest is entirely lawful, wholly honorable, and cannot by any stretch of the imagination be classed as civil disobedience. Unfortunately, this is a matter over which there has been untold confusion, and one therefore demanding specific clarification.

The American government—like most other national governments of the late twentieth century—professes democratic ideals and seeks to realize these ideals in practice. The essence of democracy is the participation of the governed in the governing process; whether direct or indirect in its mechanics, democracy is self-government. This process of general participation in policy-making supposes and indeed absolutely requires the free expression of the will of the several segments of the body politic. Universal agreement on matters of great consequence will be extremely rare in a healthy democracy. Therefore, in the formation of policy for the whole, the conflicting parties must be free to muster the evidence and present the arguments for their own sides of the case—and must be free to do so as publicly and as effectively as intelligent means permit. Nor does the democratic process cease to function once policies are formed or legislation enacted. The majority must rule, but it must not silence; critical dissent by those who find adopted laws or policies unwise or unjust must continue vigorously and without fear of reprisal. The protests of minorities, on every conceivable subject in the political sphere, is vital for the health of every democracy, from that of the township to that of the nation. Vigorous dissent must be protected and even encouraged; its substantive merit must be judged not merely by those in office but by the governing electorate in the long-term operation of their political process. In a word, genuine democracy demands dissent, thrives on protest.

The laws, institutions, and customs of American society render this theoretical approval concrete. The highest law of our land not only protects the freedom of speech categorically ("Congress shall make no law . . . abridging the freedom of speech, or of the press . . .") but specifically directs Congress to enact no legislation that would interfere with a citizen's right to petition his government for the redress of grievances. In the technical sense, and in the larger sense in which that term denotes the basic patterns of our national life, our Constitution does more than protect protest: it renders protest always legitimate and honorable for citizens of this democracy.

This supposes, of course, that whatever its political content, protest will take the form of conduct not otherwise unlawful. Speech, in written or spoken form, must be protected in all its variants. Letters and petitions of complaint to legislators, administrators, editors, are always in order. Essays in criticism, editorial attacks, formal speeches, or streetcorner harangues in bitter opposition to the policies of the government or any of its parts—all are not only permitted but valued and worthy of respect. Often protest very deeply felt will take the form of other conduct that is not verbal (or not wholly verbal) but still entirely lawful. Assemblies of protest may be convened, parades of protest organized, and picketing in public places carried on; even public prayer meetings may be held to protest some condition of pressing injustice. All of these nonverbal activities—we may call them collectively demonstrations—so long as they do not violate specific state or municipal statutes, such as traffic or trespassing ordinances, and so long as their potentially disruptive force is kept under reasonable control (clearance being received for parades in crowded public streets, and so forth), are entirely honorable forms of protest also. They may be relatively uncommon, but that is because of the efforts they entail, and their unusualness only adds to their dramatic effectiveness as protests. There is certainly nothing unlawful in doing what is unusual. Such demonstrations sometimes take forms that embarrass many citizens, or are perhaps offensive to the taste of some supporters of the policy under attack. These minor frictions are part of the costs of an operating democracy; to seek their elimination by law would be to stifle the vigorous give and take democracy requires, and would be likely to engender greater hostilities and eventually far more incendiary explosions. Demonstrations of protest are entirely lawful and appropriate devices through which an intensely concerned minority can make its voice audible, and perhaps more effective, in a political atmosphere in which noise and static may be obscuring oppressive social patterns and complacent social attitudes.

It is a serious and unjust mistake, therefore, to class all public demonstrations of protest as civil disobedience. The commonly expressed view that demonstrators—on picket lines, or marches to Washington, or the like—are engaged in a somewhat disreputable activity and are personally suspect (if not downright outlaws) only exhibits the widespread confusion in this sphere and the shallowness with which the workings of democracy are generally understood.

In some cases, however—the cases of chief interest here— demonstrations of protest do break the law. Whether those who engage in such demonstrations are for that reason worthy of condemnation or of approbation remains to be seen. In either event, unlawful demonstrations of protest are properly understood as civil disobedience and are importantly different from the rest.

6. CIVIL DISOBEDIENCE IS PUBLIC

Deliberately unlawful protest is a rough definition of civil disobedience. But there is a good deal more to it than that. An act of civil disobedience is a *public* act. For the full comprehension of civil disobedience this general, if not universal, feature of it must be appreciated. The protester, in breaking the law as he does, takes himself to be acting in the public service, not for private gain. He seeks the correction of what he takes to be a serious civic injustice. That correction can come, ultimately, only from civic action, the action of the organized community. To provoke or speed such community action, the protester knowingly decides to violate some carefully chosen law. His protest could not have the consequence he hopes for if he did not present it openly, before the public eye. In the literal sense he is seeking to *demonstrate* his conviction that gross injustice is being done, and he cannot effect this demonstration except by doing what he does in the light of the noonday sun.

Disobedient Demonstrators are sometimes criticized as being merely publicity seekers. There is usually much truth to the claim that they are seeking publicity, but it rarely if ever supports the critical sense intended in the complaint. The civil disobedient does want publicity—but he wants it for his protest and the object of his protest, not for himself. Such public attention as is given him personally is almost uniformly unfavorable and often quite damaging. He suffers that notoriety in order to bring the wrong he protests more forcefully and more clearly to the public attention.

The achievement of this end requires that his unlawful act be widely known. He will also try to make clear to the public the reasons for his disobedience, but as he will be given very little personal credence, he must hope that the forcefulness and drama of the act will render it self-explanatory. In any case, he is very unlikely to hide what he is doing. On the contrary, he is likely to make public announcement of his impending disobedience well before it takes place, at a time best calculated to receive wide public attention. For example, in *The New Statesman*, a widely read English periodical, on 17 February 1961, there appeared the following announcement: "This week-end Bertrand Russell and other demonstrators who accept the tactic of civil disobedience will take part in an unlawful protest against the Polaris missile in particular and nuclear policy in general." With this announcement was printed a short piece by Bertrand Russell explaining straightforwardly what he and his group planned to do, and why. Often the law-enforcement authorities will be specifically informed in advance of the place, time, and character of the forthcoming illegal protest. The reasons for this, however, usually go beyond the matter of publicity and will require some further attention. (See Chapter VI, Section 6.)

In some cases, of course, to give advance notice would prove self-defeating for the protester, since his efforts to begin or complete his act of protest may be blocked by police and his enterprise largely frustrated. In such cases the disobedience may be planned in such a way as to shock or disturb a complacent community, but even then publicity after the fact will be part of the goal of the demonstration.

Civil disobedience gets its name principally from the fact that it is conduct that knowingly breaks the civil law. Professor Hugo Bedau has pointed out that its name is particu-

⫹⫺ *Case 2. The deliberately public character of the act of civil disobedience is well illustrated by the symbolic and willful destruction of Selective Service registration certificates—draft cards. The act must be public if the disobedient is to have any hope of achieving his purpose. Mr. Tom Jarrell, who twice destroyed his draft card, once while serving as the target for a man throwing eggs, relates that after this latter protest, "They called me coward. I identified myself fully to the newsmen, fully aware that such open activity makes me a 'conspirator' liable to five years and/or $5,000 fine, while the man who threw the egg wouldn't identify himself, risking at most a mock charge of assault with a deadly dairy product." In his essay, "Confessions of a Two-Time Draft Card Burner" (Avatar, February 1968) he concludes:*

larly appropriate in view of the deeper sense in which it is truly *civil*. It is conduct designed to speed improvement in the civic whole, and is, as viewed by the dissenter himself, "an act that properly belongs to the public life of the community" ("On Civil Disobedience," *Journal of Philosophy*, 12 October 1961). To become a part of that public life the protest must be publicly undertaken, and the protester must suffer all the attendant consequences of public anger and personal humiliation. (See Case 2.)

7. CIVIL DISOBEDIENCE IS CONSCIENTIOUS

There are some apparent exceptions to the rule that civil disobedience must take place publicly. They are few, however, and constitute a marginal category. When (as some person or group may believe) some long-standing law or policy works great injustice on persons in some minority, and the only immediate relief possible for members of that minority can come through repeated clandestine violation of the

If the country inspires commitment, it will be supported by its people. If the government resorts to conscription, it is an indicator that it governs not a free people but a "country" that does not deserve to survive.

I am now guilty of five violations of the Selective Service laws, punishable by a maximum of 25 years in prison and/or $50,000. I intend to continue accumulating violations. When they indict Dr. Spock, they must also indict me. When they prosecute me for one transgression, they must prosecute me for all, or be guilty themselves of negligence and complicity. And if enough resisters are given life imprisonment for 20 counts each, maybe the country will discover that a draft card really is just a piece of paper. ໃ

oppressive law, we may reasonably treat such violations as cases of civil disobedience, although they are different from the main varieties of disobedient protest in that the participants conceal their activity and carefully seek to avoid arrest and punishment. One outstanding example of such special circumstances arose in the United States in the years before the Civil War, when organized bands of Northern citizens, most of whom were persons of high integrity, well-respected in their local communities, deliberately and repeatedly violated laws designed to support the slave system in the South, especially laws designed to assure the return of runaway slaves. To do so they constructed the so-called "underground railway," secreting runaway slaves by day and moving them by night until, across the Canadian border, the slaves were safe from the oppression of a grossly immoral system. To continue this practice in the interest of other, later runaways, it was essential for the managers of the underground railway to conceal their repeated violations of the fugitive slave laws.

ﾍ§ Case 3. The conscientiousness of many civil disobedients is clearly exhibited in the following Declaration of Conscience against the war in Vietnam, *in which the signatories pledged themselves to engage in civil disobedience in moral protest. (The Declaration was sponsored in 1965 by the Committee for Nonviolent Action, The Catholic Worker, the War Resisters League, and the Student Peace Union. It was reprinted in* Civil Disobedience: Theory and Practice, *ed. by Hugo A. Bedau, Pegasus Books, New York, 1969, pp. 160–61.)*

Because the use of the military resources of the United States in Vietnam and elsewhere suppresses the aspirations of the people for political independence and economic freedom;

Because inhuman torture and senseless killing are being carried out by forces armed, uniformed, trained, and financed by the United States;

Because we believe that all peoples of the earth, including both Americans and non-Americans, have an inalienable right to life, liberty, and the peaceful pursuit of happiness in their own way; and

Because we think that positive steps must be taken to put an end to the threat of nuclear catastrophe and death by chemical or biological warfare, whether these result from accident or escalation—

Concealment in such cases is a pressing tactical need, stemming from concern for the welfare of specific human beings, not from shame or remorse for the disobedient conduct. This points to another distinguishing feature of civil disobedience as a form of protest: the civil disobedient does what he does *conscientiously*, in the honest belief that what he does is right, in spite of the fact that it is illegal.

An act performed conscientiously is not necessarily objectively right or worthy of moral approval. Commonly

We hereby declare our conscientious refusal to cooperate with the United States government in the prosecution of the war in Vietnam.

We encourage those who can conscientiously do so to refuse to serve in the armed forces and to ask for discharge if they are already in.

Those of us who are subject to the draft ourselves declare our own intention to refuse to serve.

We urge others to refuse and refuse ourselves to take part in the manufacture or transportation of military equipment, or to work in the fields of military research and weapons development.

We shall encourage the development of other nonviolent acts, including acts which involve civil disobedience, in order to stop the flow of American soldiers and munitions to Vietnam.

NOTE: *Signing or distributing this Declaration of Conscience might be construed as a violation of the Universal Military Training and Service Act, which prohibits advising persons facing the draft to refuse service. Penalties of up to 5 years imprisonment and/or a fine of $5,000 are provided. While prosecutions under this provision of the law almost never occur, persons signing or distributing this declaration should face the possibility of serious consequences.*

enough men act in ways that are harmful, unjust, and even cruel, while honestly believing in their hearts that they are doing the right thing. A man's belief about the moral character of his own act is surely not the only court before which that act may be judged. But a reflective conscience is one court, and a very important one. Doing what one honestly thinks one is obligated to do is not a sufficient condition of a morally honorable act, but it is a necessary condition of such moral honor. One who does what he really believes he

ought not do (even if his act proves objectively right) is un-
true to himself, morally insincere, a hypocrite. Conscientiousness, therefore, is a feature of high moral value.

It is important to see that the civil disobedient does act
conscientiously. Having weighed the several conflicting component obligations in the context, he concludes that he must
disobey as he does, or know himself to be a hypocrite. Hypocrisy he cannot stomach. So he breaks the law, knowingly.

This is true of all civil disobedients. It must be weighed
when the aim is to evaluate their character. It helps to account for their courage in facing community scorn and legal
punishment, and their willingness to do as they do publicly.
Even for those who must hide their disobedience for practical
reasons, this conscientiousness gives to their protest a sense
of partial publicity. They will publicly assert that they are
indeed gratified that the oppressive laws in question have
been broken. To the extent that it would not interfere with
their rendering of the same service to others, they would
gladly admit their own complicity in the violations. If circumstances do not permit them to expose that conduct, at least
they take no shame in it. It is, as they believe, an act they
were morally obliged to perform. (See Case 3, pp. 20–21.)

8. CIVIL DISOBEDIENCE AND VIOLENCE

In principle, there is no specific kind of legal infraction
that civil disobedience must incorporate. The violation of
trespass or noise ordinances, deliberate traffic violations or
disturbances of the peace, refusals to obey conscription laws,
refusals to pay taxes, interferences with military preparations—any of these and a host of other deliberate unlawful

acts may serve as civil disobedience, if the essential feature of conscientious protest publicly performed is present. There is no identifiable crime called "civil disobedience." Indeed, there could be none since *it* is not a crime, although its practice must involve some crime (usually a minor one).

Whether violence may or may not play a role in civil disobedient protest is therefore a question that has no categorical answer. But the relationship between civil disobedience and violence is of considerable interest and needs to be explored.

The meaning of violence is itself unclear, but most plain men have a good idea of when it has and when it has not taken place. If I punch a policeman in the nose I am clearly violent; likewise, if I spray another person with paint or chemicals, or tip over an automobile, or set fire to a building, or stone it, I act violently. Violence supposes the use of force in ways that are directly and willfully injurious to persons or property. I am not violent when I refuse to leave some place in which I am not entitled to remain, or when I peaceably but deliberately refuse to obey some other governmental order. If I refuse to report for induction or to pay my taxes while my government wages an unjust war I am not violent. These are clear cases. There are many that are not so clear. When I lie down across a railroad track to block the movement of a train I am not violent in an ordinary sense, but that use of my body may prove to be a directly injurious one; when a group of which I am a member blocks passage to an office or building by locking arms, effectively incarcerating those within, I help to inflict some personal injury, although it may be a minor and bloodless one. The line between violence and nonviolence is not sharp but rather infinitely graded. Roughly, we take action to be violent that knowingly results in direct physical injury to persons or property. This definition, although necessarily inexact, will serve for most purposes.

The vast majority of civil disobedient protests are carefully and thoughtfully nonviolent. Partly this is because the disobedients themselves abhor violence, as good citizens everywhere do. Partly their meticulous nonviolence is a tactical requirement of their enterprise. Violence is inflammatory. Inevitably a violent protest will result in the focusing of public attention on the fact and extent of the injury done rather than upon the reason for the protest or the need to eliminate its causes. The civil disobedient, therefore, is generally very ill-advised to act violently, because such conduct will obscure the injustice he seeks to expose, and will even be used by some perpetrators of the underlying injustice to screen their own wrongs by raising hue and cry over the more obvious wrongs of the demonstrators. Violence is far more likely to hinder than to advance the purposes of civil disobedient protesters, and as a general rule they eschew it and will go to great lengths to keep their protest nonviolent.

It would be arbitrary, however, to argue, as I myself once did (in "The Essence and Ethics of Civil Disobedience," *The Nation*, 16 March 1964), that nonviolence is an *essential* element of civil disobedience. One may imagine circumstances in which a civil disobedient honestly believes himself justified in using some violence to make his protest effective. That resort to violence, however minor, will render his conduct much more difficult to justify; if the injury he does is major, or inflicted upon the person of another, it may render his conduct wholly unjustifiable, however noble his object. But the matter of justification is not immediately before us. The question here is: Can conduct that incorporates some violence ever qualify as civil disobedience? That question must be answered affirmatively; but at the same time I would reemphasize the unhappy consequences of violence for the protest itself, and the fact that civil disobedients, in actual practice, often literally *train* themselves in nonviolence and are usually the mildest and most meticulously nonviolent of men. (See Case 4.)

What circumstances might bring the protester to employ some violence? First, his immediate object being public attention, he might reason that a violent act—say the deliberate burning of an empty slum building—would, by virtue of its violence, attract greater attention, and thereby speed the accomplishment of his ultimate ends. Such reasoning is almost sure to backfire. The act certainly will receive attention, but resentment against deliberate property destruction is likely to result in a groundswell of opinion in defense of property rights, even at some cost in human welfare—the very reverse of what the disobedient protester seeks to achieve.

Second, the resort to violence may be an unfortunate but necessary element in the accomplishment of the protester's disobedient act. This will prove reasonable, if ever, only when breaking grossly unjust laws, obedience to which would result in yet greater injury—personal injury to innocents. Effecting the safety of a Jew in Nazi-occupied Holland might indeed justify the destruction of a building, or the incapacitation of a guard. If it be answered that this example relies upon a situation arising out of illegitimate and tyrannical government, the same defense of minor violence may be

✒︎❦ *Case 4. A racially integrated group known as the Committee for Nonviolent Action sponsored a Peace Walk, beginning in May 1963, from Quebec City. The Walk was to proceed through Canada, the United States, and Cuba to the U.S. Naval Base at Guantanamo Bay. All went smoothly until they reached the State of Georgia, in which they spent five months. In Griffin, Georgia, they were arrested for handing out leaflets in a park. They were tortured by electric cattle-prodders; many men and women were burnt about the face, legs and thighs, and some men about the genitals. In Macon, Georgia, they were arrested again for violating anti-leafleting laws, in defiance of repeated U.S. Supreme Court decisions that protect such distribution. Charges were eventually dropped; the walk went on. Fifteen walkers were again arrested in Albany, Georgia, for seeking to walk through the main business district of the town. In a letter to a friend one of those jailed related:*

We are involved in a difficult non-violent struggle to secure our civil liberties to walk through the center of the city and to demonstrate at Turner Air Force Base. Thirteen of us, including three

given when the object was the safety of a slave under the American government of the 1850s, or the safety of an innocent Asian peasant in the 1960s, or the safety of any innocent man from technically lawful but grossly unjust treatment, whatever the general character of the government in power.

A third possible defense of deliberate violence in protest is yet more problematical and more disturbing. Violence, some may argue, is the only language some societies can fully understand, and the only form of protest to which they will make significant response. To this argument we could shrug our shoulders in unconcern, were it the Roman conquerors of Gaul that had been so described. We cannot so easily avoid

Negroes and five white ladies, have been in jail for eighteen days. Ten have fasted completely the entire period. Another has kept a continuous fast except for one interlude with five candy bars. Six more were arrested today for demonstrating outside of City Hall for our release. . . . This is a very important non-violent struggle, not only for the integrity of the Walk, but as well for the Albany integration movement. . . . We would welcome . . . people who would like to join our witness. . . . People are needed to go to jail or to help in our office. All who come to go to jail should be prepared to stay in and fast indefinitely.

On 8 January 1964, nine of the walkers went voluntarily to Recorders Court in Albany for trial. The others refused to go to court under their own power. Some were too weak from fasting. For the first time in its history that courtroom was not racially segregated. After an eloquent statement by one of the walkers who had been fasting continuously for seventeen days, they were found guilty and sentenced to fines of 102 dollars or twenty-five days in jail, toward which the preceding days would count. Those not in court were sentenced to seven additional days for con-

it when it is the American society of the late twentieth century that is so characterized. It cannot be denied that violence plays too large a role in our national life.

Our involvement in violence on the international scene is everywhere apparent. Our recourse to the use or the threat of force, even in dealing with those much weaker than ourselves, is frequent and taken for granted. War—even war having innocent civilians as its chief victims—is often the substance of our daily news, and however much we may bemoan these facts as individuals, as a society it does not appear to disturb us deeply. With little hesitation we devote by far the greatest single portion of our national wealth to building and maintaining military forces capable of unbelievable violence, and *tempt. Some of the prisoners had to be carried out of the court on stretchers, still determined to continue their fast. Eight days later all were released. After some recuperation with friends, they resumed their walk on 27 January 1964, proceeding, as before, through the center of the Albany business district. Seventeen walkers were arrested once again, and the fast was resumed.*

Relating these events, a spokesman for the peace walkers, Mr. Tom Cornell, presented, in The Catholic Worker *(February, 1964) a moral defense of such strict nonviolence, saying, in part:*

One of the most frequent arguments against nonviolence is that it will not work in a totalitarian police state. An assumption of the nonviolent actionist is that all people are capable of responding to human suffering, especially when it is accepted voluntarily, in a sacrificial manner for the attainment of a humanitarian goal. . . . Nonviolence, however, is not merely a technique. It has as an essential component the willingness to absorb hatred and violence through the voluntary acceptance of suffering, for the benefit of the antagonist, aiming not for victory, but for a conversion, for reconciliation. There is something in every man that will respond, if we are strong enough. ૪✺

we take considerable pride in our improvement of the instruments of death, and in their successful trial. Daily we record our victories in terms of bridges and factories destroyed and the number of persons killed. We talk almost without shame about kill rates and overkill. We conscript young men into military institutions in which they are deliberately taught to be efficient killers. Honestly professing the desire for negotiated peace, we persevere in waging war until our enemies accept our terms for peace, demanding from them a submission to threat of force that we would find intolerable for ourselves. In affairs between ourselves and other nations our words are mild, but our acts are often wild.

On the local scene violence is also common. We kill each other on the highways at an incredible rate, far exceeding that of most wars. Numbers of our private citizens own guns and use them, often with tragic results. We commit more, and more violent, crimes each year than the year before, and violent disorder is now a threat in all our cities. Even our amusements have a violent tone. Professional and college sports, of absorbing interest to millions, are often physically brutal, and the most brutal, resulting in frequent public injury, is by far the most popular. Television entertainment, permeating the land, incorporates a good deal of violence; the exhibition of torture and killing is as common in programs for children as in those for adults. Filmed cartoons by which many are amused are often depictions of streams of fantasied violence; even the comic strips in the daily paper feature cruelty and bloodshed. It is hard to deny that watching or reading about humans, real and fictional, behaving brutally toward one another has become too common, too ordinary an aspect of American life.

It is in this context that some disobedient demonstrators argue that there is no alternative to communication through violence. One can see their point. The ubiquity of violence in contemporary society does render hypocritical some of the indignation with which minor property damage is generally met. How sympathetic can one be to those whose conscious political inaction, and sometimes violent community actions, inflict serious personal injury upon many—and who then display anguish when windows are broken?

Nevertheless, the argument that the greater and more despicable violence of the many justifies the lesser violence of the few is not sound. If the life of the national community is pervaded by violence, that does not at all show that effective protest must be of the same kind. On the contrary. Having little physical power, and without a hope of obtaining its objectives by sheer force, an oppressed minority that intends to be effective must devise tactics at which *it* is the master, and against which physical might is no defense. The frail and physically helpless Gandhi was successful against British power; his weapon was not armed force but moral force. Nor is it accidental that among the most effective leaders of civil disobedient protests are men of deep religious persuasion, often clergymen.

In the long run the attempt to register protest through violence is almost certain to be less effective than deliberately nonviolent methods. Violence robs the protest of its moral impact, reducing the act to the level of another crime in the streets. Moreover, in an ambiance of violence, violent acts are lost in the crowd. Protest that is carefully nonviolent, if intelligent and dramatic (and sometimes self-sacrificial), may rightly hope to speak with a more penetrating and more persuasive voice.

Finally, if the civil disobedient really has, as he professes, the goal of a peaceful and just society, he will do what he can to exhibit peacefulness and justice in his own conduct. He is likely to understand that the character of the means one employs in social action greatly influences the character of the results accomplished. The interpenetration of means and ends, their mutual support or mutual corruption, has been well understood by nonviolent activists through the generations. Referring to the American Civil War, Beriah Green, abolitionist and clergyman, wrote plainly: "We shall derive *from* the war what is characteristically involved *in* the war, and nothing else" (Carleton Mabee, *Black Freedom: The Nonviolent Abolitionists from 1830 Through the Civil War*, Macmillan, New York, 1970, p. 365). The principle applies not only to wars and their outcomes; it is more generally true that it is not possible to bring about an orderly and humane society through inhumane and disorderly conduct. Everywhere, violence in the means will infect the ends. Therefore, his object being what it is, the honorable civil disobedient has a special obligation to pursue his protest in a way that does not damage property, and certainly in a way that inflicts no direct or serious harm on any person. Most civil disobedients are acutely conscious of this obligation and manifest this consciousness in their public acts. (See Case 5.)

This is a third sense in which civil disobedience is appropriately named. It almost invariably takes the form of action that, although unlawful, is peaceable, harmless, *civilized*.

Of course a civil protest may be greeted most uncivilly. The disobedient demonstrator is likely to be presenting sensitive and controversial issues and to be approaching them in a vigorous and deliberately provocative way. The provocation, however, is essentially intellectual and emotional in nature. An agitated audience, less sophisticated than the demonstrator, may respond with physical abuse, resorting to precisely that spirit of disorder the protester had consciously avoided. Disobedient demonstrations, even when polite and peaceful, are sometimes met by an angry and violent mob. Who is to blame for personal and property damage that may then result? We must not make the common mistake of blaming the initiators of the protest. One who commits a controversial but peaceful act cannot be answerable for the unlawful response of one who witnesses the act. It is plainly wrong to

*⋙   Case 5. Exemplary is the civil disobedience of Thomas Rodd
of Pittsburgh. The history of his case appeared in a statement, "I
Stand for Them" (distributed by The Committee for Nonviolent
Action, New York, N.Y.); briefly it is this: Shortly before he became eighteen Rodd decided that he could not comply with the
conscription law or cooperate with the military system of which it
is a part. He therefore refused to register for the draft, was arrested, tried in Federal court, and convicted. Judge Louis Rosenberg gave him the choice of serving five years in prison or of
engaging, while on probation, in constructive work for a social
agency for at least two years. Conditions of this probation included the prohibition of Rodd's participation in any public
demonstration. For sixteen months Rodd complied with the
terms of the probation. His revulsion for war, however, and his
vehement but peaceful opposition to United States involvement
in Vietnam, constrained him to participate in a demonstration of
protest at the Vertol Helicopter plant near Philadelphia in December 1965. With this public action, Rodd violated, knowingly,
the conditions of his probation. On 7 January 1966, Judge
Rosenberg sentenced him to four years in Federal prison. Here
follows his statement before the court on that occasion:*

Your Honor,
One year and four months ago you and I met each other in this
building. What brought us together then was my conscientious

force all controversy and protest in a democracy to take a
form agreeable to the least sophisticated and least restrained
element of the citizenry. That path ends in the silencing of
all real controversy; it is ruinous for a democracy.

Is the disobedient demonstrator wholly unresponsible for
the violence that may follow his demonstration? That depends largely on the subsequent conduct of the demonstrators themselves. If they respond to violent attack with violent
defense, they must share the guilt, for though they did not

refusal to cooperate with our government's draft system. You came as a representative of the government, with the authority and responsibility that office implies. We are together again, and again you are here as a representative of the United States government; this time because I have openly violated the special terms of probation that you set down the last time we met. I am sorry that I have only known you in your official capacity. You and I, we are human beings—we are together, as brothers, wrapped up in this joyful confusion called life. It is presumptuous of me to say so, but I sense, and I say this in all humility, that you are a good man. I hope that you will not deny me the right to affirm our brotherhood; for in that brotherhood with all people I find the only basis for living.

You are a representative of this government, though. And often unwillingly, I, too, am a representative. With a profound feeling of inadequacy and unworthiness, I am forced by my conscience to stand as a representative of the suffering millions of Vietnam. I am forced to stand for the girl child burned to death in Bien Hoa, for the refugee cold and hungry in a camp on the outskirts of Saigon, for the weary guerilla fighter, for the Buddhist monk who is now a handful of ashes, for the thousands with no legs, thousands more with no eyes, yes, even for the U.S. Marine now slowly dying in a Philadelphia hospital. These people are my constituency. I stand for them. And my word from them to this

begin the brawl, they set the scene for it and knew what they were doing. They have a special duty not to engage in violence. If, however, the demonstrators do not respond to violence in kind but meet their attackers with disciplined and strict nonviolence, protecting themselves from physical abuse as best they can, but suffering injury without inflicting any if they must—if this is their response, they cannot be blamed for the excesses of a rampaging mob in which they have no part.

government, to this country, is this: "Stop this war! Your dominoes,
your escalation, your computer theories, your phony negotiations
are at best inhuman madness and at worst insidious, deliberate
lies. Your war, all wars, are immoral and insane. Stop it. Withdraw U.S. troops now. End the war in Vietnam!" That is the
message of my constituency. I could elaborate on and analyze their
words, because I have spent many days and weeks studying the
history of Vietnam and America's involvement there. I am not
content with slogans. I am constantly seeking new facts, new
perceptions, new theories. But I have no time for these things
now. Besides, you are a judge. You do not make our policy in
Vietnam. Even as an ordinary citizen I hazard that you have not
participated in the decisions to escalate the war. In fact, what
ordinary American citizen has? I have told you whom I represent
because that may show you why I went on a demonstration—why
I tried to stop some helicopters from going to Vietnam.

So I acted. Because my allegiance to God, my allegiance to my
conscience, my allegiance to my constituency, my integrity, de-
manded action. I seek to generate power in this witness, power to
help end the war in Vietnam. But ultimately I seek only that
power that an act of love and integrity may sometimes generate.

So here is Tom Rodd. I have tried, Lord knows, to obey this
probation. I wanted to go to Selma and walk to Montgomery—but

The self-restraint such civil disobedience requires is very
difficult to maintain. The disobedient must be prepared to
experience consequences ranging from the mildly unpleasant—verbal abuse and rotten vegetables thrown—to the
brutally painful—physical beatings and thrown rocks. In some
communities he risks being jailed indefinitely on trumped-up
charges. In a few extreme situations he may even risk being
shot. In every case the arresting officers are unlikely to be
specially gentle; he is likely to be pushed, grabbed, kicked,
twisted, tweaked, teased, and slapped. He may also have his

I didn't. I wanted to go to Washington and confront the President—but I didn't. I wanted to picket Girard College in Philadelphia—but I didn't. I wanted to help picket a non-union store on Lancaster Avenue in West Philadelphia—but I didn't. But this war is too immediate, too pressing, too terrible for me to have to say later: "but I didn't."

What about the prison term I face? It's real; it scares me. But while I face isolation my constituency faces death. My risk is miniscule compared to their reality. So if prison comes, I will accept it and make the most of it.

I have three last points: First, I have only admiration for the Federal Probation Office. Those men in this Department that I have met have been without exception fine men doing a good job. I have no beef with them or with this court. Secondly, I thank all those dear friends who have communicated with me about this action. Some differed with me, many agreed. But all were loving and kind. Last, I reiterate what anybody who knows me should know; that I am an incorrigible optimist, that I love life, and that I drink beer, play banjo, and daily toss my head and tap my feet to the romping, stomping all-pervading beat of human existence.

That's all I wanted to say, and I wish everybody a Happy New Year. ह∾

head broken with a club. From the moment his demonstration begins to the time of his release from custody, the disobedient demonstrator is certain to encounter a host of assorted indignities. Civil disobedience is not child's play.

There are not many who can submit to such physical and emotional attacks with tranquility. That being the abuse that civil disobedients must anticipate, their form of protest is understandably not generally employed. But the fact that it requires considerable courage, both physical and moral, must increase our respect for those who practice it, tending to convince us of the sincerity and depth of their commitment, and raising the political effectiveness of their acts.

This is the style of protest most characteristic of civil disobedience, and it is this strictly nonviolent conduct that should be chiefly considered when facing the question of justifiability. Some varieties of civil disobedience may employ physical violence, but they are virtually certain to be unjustifiable, except when employed against some gross and more violent tyranny. We cannot say that nonviolence is a universal and necessary feature of civil disobedience; but strict nonviolence is the archetype of civil disobedience, and it is such peaceful and civil protest with which this book is chiefly concerned.

9. THE OBJECTS OF PROTEST

By "object of protest" I mean not its objective but that against which the disobedient seeks to register his attack. There is, in principle, no limit upon the variety of these objects, and the object in any single instance certainly need not be identical with the law broken. Because certain types of objects are often assumed to be the only possible targets of disobedient demonstrations, it will be useful to distinguish the major categories into which these objects may fall.

Most commonly, the object of attack is some law of the national or local government that the demonstrator believes to be cruelly unjust. Segregation statutes in Southern states and military conscription laws are good examples. The object of protest, however, need not be a law. Almost equally common is some policy or course of action adopted by the government that the demonstrator believes to be not merely unwise but immoral. An aggressive and unjustifiable war or a severe and inequitable tax policy are examples of this. American military policy in Vietnam has probably been the object of more civil disobedience than any other political affair in our history; but the most famous single instance of civil disobedience in American history was directed against unjust taxation—The Boston Tea Party.

It is possible, but less likely, for civil disobedience to be directed against other aspects of governmental operation—against the unjust decision of an administrative body; against the appointment to a sensitive and powerful position of one known to be badly prejudiced in that sphere; or against the conviction by a military court of persons whose real offense was political opposition.

These examples, and the two major categories earlier mentioned, have this in common: all are the acts of some governmental body. Because civil disobedience is (usually) a political act primarily, it is understandable that the acts of some political agency would serve as its most appropriate targets. To the extent that civil disobedient protest can exert effective pressure, it is political figures or agencies who are most likely to be sensitive to that pressure.

But governmental acts and agencies are not the only possible objects of protest through civil disobedience. American society, for good or ill, has developed in a way that leaves many of the policy decisions affecting great masses of citizens in the hands of corporate bodies not under the direct control of government at all. Many of these institutions are exceedingly large and wealthy, and some have the most extraordinary power, not only over their own members but over the citizenry that must rely upon them for absolutely vital

services. Profit-making corporations are only one subcategory
of these—for example, retail chain stores, privately owned
utilities, steel or automobile manufacturers. Beyond these
are the great labor unions, influential fraternal and charitable
organizations, and giant private philanthropic foundations. In
all of these, and others, private corporate bodies make decisions that, if ill-considered or unjust, may cause great anguish, both to individuals and to relatively weak minorities.
It is not surprising, therefore, that civil disobedience should,
on occasion, have as its object the acts or policies of some
such private bodies.

Two excellent illustrations of this tendency have been witnessed in recent years:

(a) One of the most degrading aspects of the policy of
racial segregation so widely applied in Southern states was
that of refusing to serve blacks at lunch counters and in
restaurants where whites customarily dined. This mealtime
discrimination had some support in local ordinances forbidding racial mixing, but the regulation was largely im-
plemented and maintained by the privately owned stores and
restaurants whose owners either agreed with that policy or
accepted it out of a supposed economic necessity. One of the
great turning points in the civil rights movement came as the
result of organized demonstrations of protest, some lawful
but many disobedient, against the policies of these private
restaurant managers. The now famous "lunch-counter sit-ins"
resulted in much immediate tension, many arrests, and a
great deal of harassment on both sides. But more than anything else these sit-ins pricked the conscience of the nation,
and (perhaps more importantly) they pricked the conscience

of those who patronized those same chain-restaurants in more populous Northern cities. The combination of economic and moral pressure had speedy results. The policy of lunch-counter segregation in these chain stores, and in most of the larger private establishments of the South, had to be scrapped.

(b) The opening of the New York World's Fair of 1963 was attended by large scale civil disobedience, in the form of traffic violations, the object of which was the racially discriminatory policies in force among the construction crews on the Fair grounds. Some blamed the building trades unions; others blamed the private contractors themselves. The causes, and even the facts of the case have been much disputed, and the disobedient protest itself had little positive effect, if any. In this case, as in the former one, no governmental act or agency but the policies of private and powerful corporate institutions were the object of protest. As such institutions continue to grow in size and influence, their power often exceeding their wisdom, we may expect civil disobedience directed against them to increase in frequency and in fervor.

10. SUMMARY: A DEFINITION OF CIVIL DISOBEDIENCE

"Civil disobedience" is an expression rather loosely used, having a wide range of applications; any attempt at precise definition is therefore bound to be somewhat arbitrary. Its most essential and most common features, however, we can now identify.

Civil disobedience is an act of protest, deliberately unlawful, conscientiously and publicly performed. It may have as its object the laws or policies of some governmental body, or those of some private corporate body whose decisions have serious public consequences; but in either case the disobedient protest is almost invariably nonviolent in character.

The spirit of civil disobedience is one of sacrificial service to the community, and that spirit is more central to it than is the technical form of the protest, for the form may vary with the circumstances, but the aim of community service does not. Martin Luther King, the most distinguished defender of civil disobedience, achieved his greatness by embodying that spirit in his own life. In 1964, accepting the Nobel Peace Prize in Oslo, Dr. King said:

The nonviolent resisters can summarize their message in the following simple terms: We will take direct action against injustice despite the failure of governmental and other official agencies to act first. We will not obey unjust laws or submit to unjust practices. We will do this peacefully, openly, cheerfully, because our aim is to persuade. We adopt the means of nonviolence because our end is a community at peace with itself. We will try to persuade with our words, but if our words fail, we will try to persuade with our acts. We will always be willing to talk and seek fair compromise, but we are ready to suffer when necessary and even risk our lives to become witnesses to the truth as we see it. [The New York Times, 12 December 1964.]

WHAT CIVIL DISOBEDIENCE IS NOT

1. NOT EVERY PUBLIC DEMONSTRATION IS CIVIL DISOBEDIENCE

It will be clear from what has gone before (see Chapter I, Section 4) that most protest, however vehement or unusual, is not civil disobedience and would be improperly classified as such. Because civil disobedience necessarily involves some deliberate infraction of the law, all parades, assemblies, marches, picket lines, and other public demonstrations that abide by the law are *not* civil disobedience. Such lawful protests also need to be evaluated; they also may be foolish, wrongheaded, or (even if well motivated) tactically ill-advised. But public demonstrations of protest, as such, are not disobedient and are not our present subject.

2. CONSCIENTIOUS OBJECTION IS NOT CIVIL DISOBEDIENCE

Civil disobedience must be conscientiously performed (see Chapter I, Section 7); that is, it must flow from the principled and deeply held convictions of the protester. But "conscientious objection" is a special expression, generally reserved to identify a special device of the body politic. This device usually takes the form of a clause in certain legislation that makes it possible for those who find the acts that law requires morally intolerable to comply with the law in some alternative (and to them morally unobjectionable) way. Its most common, but not exclusive, use is in conscription legislation, under which religious pacifists or other categories of conscientious objectors may apply for permission to render an equivalent period of social service to the state in some welfare organization of a noncombatant, and usually nonmilitary character. The conscientious objector—whether or not he is right in his repugnance for all military activity—acts entirely within the provisions of the law. He follows procedures specified by statute and is protected by the law once his status as conscientious objector is administratively established. He must not be viewed as a violator of the law; his conduct certainly is not civil disobedience.

It is also true that some persons deliberately violate the selective service laws out of sincere respect for moral principles. Their acts *are* instances of civil disobedience. Although truly motivated by conscience, such persons are not properly classed as "conscientious objectors" as that expression is most generally used. Conscientious objection, in the normal sense, may be considered a form of protest, but it is never disobedient.

3. CIVIL DISOBEDIENCE IS NOT REVOLUTION

Revolution seeks the overthrow of constituted governmental authority, or at least repudiates that authority in some sphere; civil disobedience does neither. This distinction is of the most fundamental importance in understanding civil disobedience and in appraising it.

In certain circumstances, of course, even revolution may prove justifiable. Of the countless revolutions that have transpired in human history, many are the culmination of a process in which an exploited mass throws off what they believe to be their oppressive yoke; some are the work of a dedicated minority acting on behalf of the masses. We Americans think our colonial forefathers were justified in rebelling against the British Crown, and so likewise the loyal citizens of many nations believe their nationhood owed to the courage and wisdom of their revolutionary founders. In France, in Mexico, in China, and Ireland, and Cuba, and in a hundred other lands, "the Revolution" is regarded as the event of greatest national honor, and the revolutionaries are gloried and revered. Of course, revolutionaries are traitors. Their treason is against an authority they believe illegitimate or cruel; nevertheless it is high crime, and when the rebel is caught he is likely to be executed. But if the act accuse, the result will excuse—provided, as Machiavelli carefully points out—that the rebel is successful. If he is, he may become the Father of his Country. Revolution is the classic case in which—at least so far as the official history of the nation will record—military success assures moral justification. Might does not make right; but in some circumstances it produces a very persuasive synthetic.

Viewed objectively, of course, some revolutions have been justified and some have not. Oppressive cruelty has not been rare in human history, and the appeal to arms to end it may sometimes have been the only recourse left. Which cases are truly of that sort? The Algerian? The Bolivian? The Indo-

..e American? Reliable answers require the most
..eful historical study of particular cases, and even then are
never beyond doubt. Some revolutions, on the other hand,
seek the overthrow of a reasonably stable and generally decent government and advance chiefly the private interests of
the revolutionaries. "Governments long established should not
be changed," as the American revolutionaries who signed the
Declaration of Independence wisely agreed, "for light and
transient causes." Revolutions are too serious to be undertaken lightly. Almost invariably they spill human blood; sometimes, as in the American and Spanish civil wars, revolutions
bequeath a legacy of misery and bitterness that cannot be
forgotten for decades, or even a century. He who revolts
against the constituted authority, whatever his reasons, necessarily unsettles the life of the entire community, shakes the
security and peace of mind of all its members, brings on great
loss of property, and renders probable the injury and death
of many human beings. Revolution tears up the fabric of a
nation's life; justified or not it is an awful thing.

Civil disobedience is another matter entirely. It does not
result in death or misery and rarely entails significant loss of
property. It does not seek to unseat an existing government
and does not destroy the order or stability of national or
community life. It *is* a serious matter, in being a deliberate
violation of the law, but it is a shallow (although common)
mistake to confuse it with revolution or to view the civil disobedient as a revolutionary.

The essential difference between the two lies in this: the
civil disobedient does, while the revolutionary does not, accept the general legitimacy of the established authorities.
While the civil disobedient may vigorously condemn some

law or policy those authorities institute, and may even refuse to comply with it, he does not by any means intend to reject the larger system of laws of which that one is a very small part. In accepting that system he accepts even the technical legitimacy of the law he breaks; he recognizes that in one very important sense that law does claim obedience from him, and he knows that his defiance of that claim—while he accepts the general legitimacy of the system—requires some special justification. In short, the civil disobedient acts deliberately within the framework of established political authority; the revolutionary seeks to demolish that framework, or to capture it. The difference is monumental.

Two great men, both alleged practitioners of civil disobedience, may be more fully understood in the light of this distinction. The first, Henry David Thoreau, wrote the most famous of all essays on the subject: "On the Duty of Civil Disobedience" (1849). He also refused to pay taxes lawfully imposed. The object of his attack was twofold: the American prosecution of an unjust war with Mexico and, more especially, the American retention of a system of human slavery. His conduct—deliberate violation of the law and submission to arrest without resistance—is typical of civil disobedients. His essay makes it very clear, however, that what he intended was not merely protest but the complete repudiation of governmental authority. He wished the government to "treat him as a neighbor," to recognize him as a "higher and independent power." He said:

How does it become a man to behave toward this American government today? I answer that he cannot without disgrace be associated with it. I cannot for an instant recognize that political organization as my government which is the slaves' government

*also. . . . I quietly declare war with the State, after my fashion,
though I will still make what use and get what advantage of her
I can, as is usual in such cases. . . . I think that it is not too
soon for honest men to rebel and revolutionize.*

Thoreau's act may have been a noble one, but in placing
himself above the law and denying its jurisdiction over him,
he became a rebel. Although his essay probably introduced
the expression into common speech, Thoreau himself did
not, in the strict sense, defend civil disobedience.

The second, Mahatma Gandhi, was one of history's most
effective leaders, and the greatest exponent of the technique
of "passive resistance," *satyagraha.* Gandhi's movement was
exceedingly subtle and complex, but one aspect of it needs
clarification for our purposes. He sought to develop and
strengthen moral resistance to the British rule of India, and
to do so wholly without force of arms. His strictly nonviolent
methods often incorporated disobedience of some British law
or decree, but it was the spiritual resistance, not the disobedience as such, that was the leading character of his acts;
prolonged hunger strikes that served as symbolic defiance of
British authority were more typical of him than deliberate
legal infractions. Most important, the entire movement aimed
at, and accomplished, the destruction of British authority in
the land. Although the transfer of authority did come, at last,
in a peaceful way, that transfer was the culmination of a
genuinely revolutionary movement, of which Gandhi was
the known and self-conscious leader. Gandhi was a rebel; had
tactical considerations permitted, he would surely have been
permanently banished or executed. That he was not was due
to the special reverence with which he was regarded by the

Indian masses, and his consequent political power. It is therefore quite misleading to treat Gandhi as a civil disobedient exclusively. To do so is to err on both sides, missing first the fundamental nature of his aims and achievements, and supposing second that civil disobedience typically seeks the overthrow of established authority.

Still, the history of Gandhi's movement is evidence that although revolution and civil disobedience are conceptually distinct, it is in some cases difficult to draw a sharp line of distinction between them. He who seeks the destruction of one system of government and its replacement by another is a revolutionary; but in the slow process of building that revolution he may practice and encourage civil disobedience directed against specific acts of oppression. In this, as in every case of moral significance, what a man is *doing* depends importantly not only upon his external deeds but also upon his internal intentions. These intentions are difficult to determine in some cases—as criminal lawyers know well—but in many cases they are reasonably clear. There was never much doubt that Gandhi's intent was revolutionary; he said so quite straightforwardly. In a similar but not so obvious way, some of those who practice civil disobedience in America or Great Britain may have long-range revolutionary hopes. But their hopes are one thing and their concrete acts are another. A just government must be always meticulous in prosecuting at law only established infractions of the law, not fantasy or deluded political ambition.

The great majority of civil disobedients, in any event, leave no doubt about their real intentions. They abjure revolution, and, although sometimes angry at their government, they make it very clear that their act is one committed *under* the law, even if against it. In one sense revolution is the furthest thing from their minds. Their object—pursued with self-sacrificial vigor—is not to replace the system but to improve it.

4. CIVIL RIOTS ARE NOT CIVIL DISOBEDIENCE

Riots have become a serious threat in large American cities. Periodic onsets of civil chaos have recently become much more frequent and much more destructive than ever before, creating a widely felt sense of national insecurity and disorder. The causes of these social paroxysms lie very deep—in history, in the selves of their participants, and in the structure of the society that gives birth to them. Linking these fundamental causes with the riots themselves are a set of intermediate disorders that are both ugly and humiliating: rotten housing, bad schools, broken families, general filth, and a widespread feeling of powerlessness and alienation. These are running sores on the body politic. Leaders of all parties talk much about the need to heal them, but in fact very little is being accomplished toward that end; the fundamental causes are little understood and rarely dealt with. Minor patches of improvement emerge here and there, with fairer employment practices and more public housing, but the infection still spreads in the Nation, showing new and ever more virulent symptoms.

The riot is one way—violent, destructive, and irrational, but for many concrete and satisfying—of reacting against a set of social injustices for which we seem to have no forseeable effective remedy and no rational problem-solving system that promises remedy. It is important to differentiate these unhappy outbreaks of disorder from civil disobedience.

In the first place, civil disobedience, unlike riots, is not violent or destructive (see Chapter I, Section 8), and even the slightest use of physical force directly against persons or property will be avoided wherever possible. Nonviolence is usually a principle of importance to the civil disobedient; rampant violence is anathema to him and is inconsistent with both the strategy and the objective of his protest.

In the second place, civil disobedience, unlike riots, is (whether or not it proves ultimately justified) a rational tactic, intellectually chosen and pursued. It is undertaken thoughtfully and deliberately, with careful limits self-imposed. The civil disobedient breaks the law, but he does not disregard it; his acts are coolly and calmly performed and are never, as civil riots are, sheer bursts of passion or blind ventings of fury. In its tranquility, forethoughtfulness, and ultimate respect for authority, civil disobedience is as much unlike civil rioting as anything can be.

There are, it is true, some features in common. Both violate the law. Both are, in some rough sense, protests, and the object of attack is sometimes the same general sort of injustice —racial discrimination, felt oppression. But the differences are more important than the likenesses. Riots, in the final analysis, are revolutionary in intent. Their participants do not—at least for that time in that place—accept the legitimacy of the authorities or their laws. They have no real plan for the replacement of these authorities by another, and probably no serious intention of forming such a plan. To that degree their revolt is partial and chaotic, and doomed to accomplish little but destruction. A revolt it is, nevertheless. The law is blatantly defied. Looting, arson, mad rampaging, and even beatings and deadly assaults, follow one another without reason, not in a spirit of civic dedication but in that of fiery anger, and with exultation that the chains of "the system" are, at least for a few wild hours or days, defiantly cast aside, without apparent danger of arrest or punishment.

Rioting is a kind of civic madness. Of course the sickness is no more to be cured with tanks and guns than is the sickness of insanity cured by the use of a strait-jacket. In both cases the patient may be quieted until he regains his senses; but in both cases the repeated and severe application of physical restraint is likely to increase hostility and alienation, providing yet more fuel for the next fire. In neither case does sheer force even approach the roots of the malady.

The riots that have beset American cities, and promise to continue to do so, are, in a word, uprisings. The descriptive term used by the participants themselves, and their leaders, is *rebellion*. That is on the whole an accurate description, and it clearly marks off these disorders from all varieties of civil disobedience.

~§ III §~

THE KINDS OF CIVIL DISOBEDIENCE

1. SYSTEMS OF CLASSIFICATION

Instances of civil disobedience vary enormously, not only in the special features of the acts themselves and their contexts but also with regard to the principles upon which they proceed. A rough classification of the major kinds of civil disobedience will be very helpful in understanding particular protests.

How the kinds of civil disobedience are classified depends, of course, upon the purposes of the classifier. Where the chief concern is a judgment upon the act itself, its rightness or wrongness, we will sort by features that bear on the objective justifiability of the protest. Where the greater interest is in the character of the disobedient protesters, their goodness or badness, we will sort by features that bear upon their motivation, and their ethical or political orientation.

None of these categories can be sharply defined, of course, and the two major systems of classification can be superimposed on one another, resulting in some complication. But some sorting is essential for the rational discussion and evaluation of individual cases.

2. DIRECT AND INDIRECT CIVIL DISOBEDIENCE

All cases of civil disobedience fall pretty clearly into one of two categories, which may be called *direct* and *indirect.* Direct civil disobedience is an act in which the law deliberately broken *is itself* the object of the protest. Indirect civil disobedience includes all the rest, in which the law broken *is other than* (although more or less closely related to) the object of protest.

Some illustrations: suppose a Caucasian deliberately sits in the Negro waiting room of a legally segregated bus station, with the clear aim of protesting that segregation statute. Or suppose a man protests against the injustice of some conscription law by deliberately refraining from any cooperation with those who administer it and publicly announcing his refusal to register for conscription in the manner specifically prescribed by law. These are cases in which the law broken and the object of protest are identical; the protest is direct. Suppose, on the other hand, that a group deliberately violates some trespass law in demonstration against the testing of some nuclear weapons. Or suppose, to dramatize the indecency of the war in Vietnam, a lone protester disrobes entirely on a public street and once naked parades with a sign reading "I am not obscene, but the war is!" His legal offense is against some statute forbidding indecent exposure, while the object of his concern is national or international policy. Such cases of civil disobedience are indirect.

Direct civil disobedience, whether or not one believes it sometimes justifiable, is at least readily and generally understood as being the protest it is intended to be. Indirect civil disobedience is very commonly misunderstood and therefore calls for some further comment.

The very feature causing some instances of civil disobedience to be called indirect—separateness of the act from the object of its attack—creates problems for its practitioners that are difficult to overcome. They must somehow make clear to an apathetic or hostile public what the connection is between their disobedience and their social concern. Indirect disobedience is the more effective, therefore, when that connection is most immediately evident, most easily grasped. Some symbolic relationship between the two will usually be sought. This symbolic tie may spring from the *location* of the disobedient act (e.g., in the Selective Service office, or on the site of segregated construction work), or from the *time* of the disobedience (e.g., deliberately blocking traffic on the anniversary of some fateful event), or from the *nature* of the disobedient act (e.g., pouring oil mixed with feathers on the floor of the main offices of an oil company responsible for much coastline pollution). These devices may be combined, as in pouring blood on the records in Selective Service offices, and so on. In some measure the relationship between the act of indirect civil disobedience and the object of protest must be purely conventional—established only for the purpose of that protest. But it is essential for the success of the protest that these relationships, symbolic and conventional, be widely understood by members of the community in which the protest takes place. To this end the connection must not be wholly arbitrary, and it rarely is. (See Case 6.)

Indirect disobedience will normally prove much harder to justify than direct disobedience, other things being equal.

∎§   *Case 6. Indirect civil disobedience, relying upon the symbolic use of napalm and fire at a Selective Service Board office, is dramatically illustrated by the following actual case. Daniel and Philip Berrigan, brothers and Catholic priests, together with seven others (known collectively as the Catonsville Nine) publicly took records from a Maryland draft board office and burned them to protest the war in Vietnam. Before this act of civil disobedience, in the fall of 1968, Father Berrigan wrote a justificatory statement, later published in* The Michigan Daily *(12 October 1968). It reads in part:*

Some 10 or 12 of us (the number is still uncertain) will, if all goes well (ill?) take our religious bodies during this week to a draft center in or near Baltimore. There we shall, of purpose and forethought, remove the 1-A files, sprinkle them in the public street with homemade napalm, and set them afire. For which act we shall, beyond doubt, be placed behind bars for some portion of our natural lives, in consequence of our inability to live and die

How difficult the justification of a particular act of civil disobedience will be must depend, in part, upon how dramatic and how generally understood is the symbolic connection between the law broken and the object of protest. The justification of civil disobedience may depend upon its effectiveness, and its effectiveness (when indirect) will be much affected by the clarity of the relationship between symbol and object. As the law to be disobeyed is chosen more arbitrarily, or is more distantly or more uncertainly connected to the object of protest, effectiveness, and with it justifiability, may drop sharply.

Appropriateness of the relation of act to object is not the only factor bearing on justifiability; a host of others remain to be discussed (see Chapter VI, Section 6). In all cases of content in the plagued city, to say "peace, peace" when there is no peace, to keep the poor poor, the homeless, the thirsty, and hungry homeless, thirsty, and hungry.

Our apologies, good friends, for the fracture of good order, the burning of paper instead of children, the angering of the orderlies in the front parlor of the charnel house. We could not, so help us God, do otherwise. For we are sick at heart; our hearts give us no rest for thinking of the Land of Burning Children. . . . You must bear with us, for His sake. Or if you will not, the consequences are our own. . . .

The war in Vietnam is more and more literally brought home to us. Its inmost meaning strikes the American ghettos; in servitude to the affluent. We must resist and protest this crime.

Finally, we stretch out our hands to our brothers throughout the world. We who are priests, to our fellow priests. All of us who act against the law turn to the poor of the world, to the Vietnamese, to the victims, to the soldiers who kill and die, for the wrong reasons, for no reason at all, because they were so ordered

indirect civil disobedience, however, a widely understood linkage between the disobedient act and the object of concern is a necessary condition (although not a sufficient one) of that disobedience being proved justifiable.

One point remains to be emphasized. It is wrong to maintain that cases of indirect civil disobedience cannot be justified *because* the law broken is not the object of protest. To argue so is to beg the central question. If it will be granted that civil disobedience may, at some times or under some circumstances, prove justifiable, it remains to be seen what those circumstances are, and what forms that disobedience might reasonably take. There may be situations in which disobedient protest is called for, while direct disobedience is simply out of the question. For example, if the object of a

—by the authorities of that public order which is in effect a massive institutionalized disorder.

We say: killing is disorder, life and gentleness and community and unselfishness is the only order we recognize. For the sake of that order, we risk our liberty, our good name. The time is past when good men can remain silent, when obedience can segregate men from public risk.

We ask our fellow Christians to consider in their hearts a question which has tortured us, night and day, since the war began. How many must die before our voices are heard? How many must be tortured, dislocated, starved, maddened? How long must the world's resources be raped in the service of legalized murder? When, at what point, will you say no to this war?

We have chosen to say, with the gift of our liberty, if necessary our lives: the violence stops here, the death stops here, the suppression of the truth stops here, this war stops here. . . .

Redeem the times! The times are inexpressibly evil. . . . 🙠

protest is to be the conduct of a war, or another issue of national policy, it may be impossible for the protester to violate that policy directly. So also if the object of protest is not a law but the absence of a law, or some other administrative nonfeasance, direct civil disobedience would be impossible. It does not follow, of course, that in such cases indirect civil disobedience is automatically justified, but neither can it be automatically condemned.

3. MORAL AND POLITICAL CIVIL DISOBEDIENCE

A full understanding of any actual instance of civil disobedience requires an appreciation of the motivation of the disobedient. For this we must go beyond the analysis of the objectively performed act, inquiring into the subjective and hence murky sphere of the character and aims of the actor. Civil disobedience is in every case the act of a conscientious person; but the particular principles to which that person believes himself bound by conscience will shed much light upon his entire enterprise, and upon him.

Human motivation is rarely simple. Behind the act of the most honest and scrupulous civil disobedient are likely to lie a number of intertwined motivating principles; about some the disobedient himself may be unconscious or unclear. Determining the "real" motivation in a particular case is therefore a messy and uncertain business. But often one can arrive at some fair judgment in this matter, usually with the candid help of the protester himself. He is not ashamed of his act and will often express as clearly as he can, to whomever will listen, his principled reasons for disobedience. Both the appraisal of his character and the understanding of situations in which disobedient protest is employed will be aided by a classification of the kinds of motivation that are commonly operative in such situations.

Moral motivation and *political* motivation are the two major categories. No false division between moral and political affairs is intended here. Political acts *are* moral acts, having moral consequences and deserving moral judgment. Politicians or political theorists who think they can pursue their business clear of all moral commitments are seriously mistaken. Planning and theorizing without regard for moral principles often results in plans and theories in conflict with the moral principles that ought to have informed and guided them. In political affairs an activity purportedly *a*moral usually turns *im*moral at last. Political decisions are decisions affecting the body politic—and that body consists of human beings whose happiness and well-being is an affair of the highest moral import. Politics and morals cannot be separated.

But they can be distinguished. Some acts and decisions take place within an essentially political framework, being addressed primarily to the whole community in view of its common concerns. Other acts and decisions are more specifically personal, being undertaken by a man for himself, out of chief regard for principles and values that he accepts as governing his conduct. These latter often have political import—import for the whole community—just as the former have moral import. But in being differently conceived and differently aimed, the two kinds of acts may reasonably be distinguished from one another, the first called political, the second moral.

Civil disobedience may be chiefly political or chiefly moral in character. Although in practice it is sometimes hard to draw the distinction, it is of considerable interest. Political civil disobedience is much the more common. It is disobedience specifically addressed to the members of the community at large and intended to influence their subsequent conduct. The reasons for seeking such influence may be deeply ethical, of course, but the objective sought by the protest is the repeal or passage of legislation, the change of government or business policy, or the like. Political civil disobedience aims to achieve some result of importance in the *polis*. Its effectiveness must be judged by the extent to which the protest speeds or otherwise advances that envisaged change. Its justification may depend upon the likelihood of its having such political consequences.

Moral civil disobedience is less ambitious; it is more limited in object, more specific in intent. He whose civil disobedience is moral may also wish for the change or elimination of some law or policy he believes to be unjust. But his disobedient act is not so much a device to effect that change as it is a public statement of his (the disobedient's) inability to comply in good conscience. Moral civil disobedience is the protester's response to a direct conflict between his personal ethical principles and some law of the state. It may or may not have some tendency to produce a desired political change. If it does, so much the better, the moral disobedient may say; if it does not, or has even the opposite effect, that will be regrettable—but the disobedient act he is obliged to perform in either case. (See Case 7). The basic considerations for him are not the results to which the disobedience leads but the principles upon which it is grounded. Political disobedience is essentially public; moral disobedience may or may not be performed in public.

Political civil disobedience is essentially a *tactic*. Whether it be a good tactic depends upon what is likely to ensue, in a given case, from its practice—whether the long-range goals of its practitioners are advanced. Moral civil disobedience is the concrete outcome of some deep ethical convictions. Its tactical functions are secondary at best, and its practitioners may reply to the objection that it will not prove a wise move simply by saying that that is unfortunate but beyond their control.

One illustration of moral civil disobedience (or the intent to commit it) is the deliberate response made by Ralph Waldo Emerson upon reading the Fugitive Slave Law of 1850. He said: "By God, I will not obey it." Another exam-

✍ *Case 7. Moral civil disobedience is well illustrated by the following two cases:*

(a) Robert Gilliam, a pacifist and devout Catholic, pleaded guilty in Minneapolis Federal Court to the charge of refusing induction into military service. In his statement to the Court before sentencing, on 14 August 1967, Gilliam said: "The state wants my body to make war. I am here today because I have refused it. I have refused to cooperate with Selective Service because conscription is a war institution." The presiding judge commended Gilliam for his good record as a student and for his serious desire for peace. He then said: "Yet you have pleaded guilty, and I feel I do have to impose a prison penalty. But I am sure you will use your time well." Gilliam was sentenced to two years in a federal penitentiary. In an earlier letter to his family and friends, reprinted in The Catholic Worker (September 1967), he had written:

This is a hard letter to write. I want to try to explain to you all a decision I have made. I have decided to discontinue cooperation with Selective Service. . . . In my letter to Selective Service I said that "conscription is a war institution, its purpose is to organize young men for war making. To cooperate with Selective

ple is the oldest case of civil disobedience on record. It is reported in Exodus (1:15–20) that when the king of Egypt commanded the Hebrew midwives to kill all the male infants of the Hebrew women, the midwives deliberately disobeyed: "But the midwives feared God, and did not as the king of Egypt commanded them, but saved the men children alive."

Instances of political civil disobedience have become reasonably frequent in American life, taking many different forms, depending upon what is believed likely, under the given circumstances, to prove most effective. Several major varieties of political civil disobedience can be sorted out, their distinguishing characteristics being the different ways in

Service is to support war. I wish instead to make clear my total rejection of war and to withdraw my support in every possible way." . . . Reverend Maurice McCracklin [a Cincinnati minister who was secretary of the No Tax for War Committee] says, "That Jesus would participate in or lend his willful support to violence and war is to me unthinkable. Therefore if I am loyal to Him I will oppose war and the spirit that makes for war to the limit of my ability." You don't have to extend much beyond the actual words of Jesus to see that a Christian cannot support war. It seems to me that a Christian is called to love all his brothers, indiscriminately, as Jesus loved; he is called to serve, to return good for evil, to be a peacemaker, and to have faith in love as the force which conquers.

(b) Thomas S. Hathaway, an American student who refused the order to report for induction, explained why he did so in a letter reprinted in The Catholic Worker *(February 1967). The letter reads, in part: "The reason I will not go into the army is that I will not kill another person. Nor will I take part in the activities and support of an institution whose purpose is to provide men who will kill when someone decides it is necessary."* ৯৯

which the disobedient act is employed to bring about the desired political result.

First and most important is civil disobedience of *pressure*. Here the object is to prod the legislature, or the executive, or the corporate managers, or whoever has the power to make the desired change, into making it. The disobedients aim to force those in positions of influence and authority into action by public embarrassment. For disobedience of pressure to be effective, the law or policy that is the object of its attack must embody an injustice reasonably clear to anyone who reflects upon it. Believing the law at issue to be such, the disobedient reasons that to achieve his political objectives his instrument must be one that will force the legislature (or other responsible body) to reflect; he must break some law in a way that will make the object of protest a focal point of sustained attention. Once that that is achieved, he may argue, a reasonably healthy democratic process will take care of the matter through normal channels. Reliance need not be placed upon the good character of officeholders, although such character may help. Officeholders are no less moral than ordinary citizens. Indeed, legislators are often more sensitive than their constituents to considerations of moral obligation or welfare needs and are for that reason particularly vulnerable to the pressure of civil disobedience that has a morally just objective. But even if the legislature or executive has pursued some unjust policy out of selfish interests, or allowed it to continue out of moral insensitivity, those who elect them will feel the prick of conscience (the disobedient argues) when fellow citizens sacrifice themselves in deliberate disobedience. The recurrent need for popular support will compel those in power to effect some political remedy.

Of course the disobedient demonstrators may be in error about the amount of pressure their disobedience can bring to bear, and they may even be in error about the alleged injustice they seek to alleviate. But this, in any event, is the general theme of their protest: compel the public and the powers that be to *see* the wrongs they now enforce, and such wrongs will soon be righted. Civil disobedience of pressure is more likely to be effective when the operating principles of the government are democratic, and where the wrong in question is within the power of the people's deputies to remedy. But it may be employed even against authoritarian leaders to the extent that they rely upon a mass following, and may be directed also against the policies of privately owned corporations or other nongovernmental bodies when such institutions find it important to retain public good will.

The pressure employed here, of course, is not physical or economic but ethical and electoral; again politics and morals intertwine. The demonstrators reason that, to retain the political support of their constituents, the authorities will react to the exposure of injustice in the existing scheme. But, unless the authorities feel that moral pressure internally, the exertion of pressure requires not only that the masses of the electorate share the ethical principles of the protesters but that they be made explicitly conscious of these principles, and of the current violations of them. To accomplish this, publicity is absolutely essential; and to achieve maximal publicity deliberate violation of law may be the surest and best device. Massive protests against policies of racial discrimination have often taken this deliberately disobedient form—in sit-ins, freedom rides, and the like. The injustice protested being genuine and severe, the forcing of it upon the nation's attention was an effective device in promoting some remedies. Much of the credit for the important civil rights legislation in the United States during the 1960s, however incomplete as remedies, is owed to courageous civil disobedients who helped build up the necessary pressure. Most of these demonstrators were punished, formally or informally, some with great severity. But they forced their countrymen to begin to see what injustice had been going on so long under their noses. Their civil disobedience was political in form, though morally inspired, and it was often effective.

A second variety, also political in conception, is civil disobedience of *confrontation*. This, too, is a form of pressure,

but it seeks to be effective more directly. Where the protesters are convinced that the existing authorities will not
respond to the exposure of injustices—either because they
are evil men or (more likely) because they have developed a
distorted conception of the actual state of affairs, and hence
deny the facts or badly misinterpret them—the disobedience
may have as its objective a kind of political shock treatment.
The leaders (it is argued) must be stunned, provoked, awak-
ened. Reasoned pleas and petitions having proved hopeless,
the protesters believe that they must force the government to
see how deadly serious their protest is. Perhaps by direct
confrontation with a self-sacrificing mass the leaders will
awaken at last, or will at least, perhaps out of fright, amend
their policy so as to mitigate its injustice. Assemblies of protest are often confrontations, but assemblies alone are wholly
lawful and are too easily ignored. Hence the assembled mass
must perform a deliberately unlawful act, perhaps a shocking
one, not with the aim (as is the case with an unscrupulous
few) of deliberately provoking police violence but in order
to compel attention and perhaps bring about a re-thinking
of policy.

Characteristic of disobedience of confrontation is the large
size of the demonstration; the greater the mass of demonstrators the more likely they are to have the shocking effect
sought. Hence the arguments, after the demonstration, over
how many actually did participate—both sides (protesters and
authorities) often exaggerating (and sometimes lying) about
the number of participants, in order to make the protest appear more (or less) significant than it really was. The location of such disobedience is of special importance too, for the
setting must be one in which the demands of the demonstra-

✍ *Case 8. On 21 and 22 October 1967, some scores of thousands of Americans assembled in Washington and marched from the Lincoln and Washington Monuments to the Pentagon, which, as headquarters of the U.S. Department of Defense, was the symbol of the war in Vietnam so bitterly opposed. During the afternoon of the 22nd, a considerable number of those surrounding the Pentagon staged a deliberately illegal sit-in to pursue their protest, moving thereby from confrontation in the form of lawful assembly to civil disobedience through confrontation. The impact of these confrontations was considerable.*

A circular promoting the demonstration, distributed by the National Mobilization Committee, one of the organizing groups, read in part: "Support Our Men in Vietnam! Bring Them Home Now—Alive! Stop the War Machine!" And the circular was headed:

CONFRONT THE WARMAKERS
WASHINGTON, D.C.

tors are absolutely forced upon the attention of legislators or administrators directly. Disobedient confrontations will therefore require much planning and preparatory logistical work and will be scheduled in Washington, some state capital, or another very public place. (See Case 8.) Another form of this tactic, sometimes disobedient, is that of confrontation between protesters and candidates for high office during their election campaigns—making it awkward if not impossible for the candidate to refuse some response, and sometimes even making it difficult for the campaign to proceed as scheduled. The candidate is thereby compelled to face the issue of concern to the protesters and to do so while the focus of public attention is upon him.

A third and extreme variety of civil disobedience is *re-*

sistance. Here too the object is to force the change of policy by action that is direct and shocking. But in this case the disobedients have also the parallel aim of doing whatever they can to reduce the effectiveness of the unjust law or policy in question. To this end they act in a way that is openly and deliberately disruptive: blocking the path of government agents, clogging government offices with their own bodies, physically obstructing access to military induction centers, counseling others to disobey the laws believed unjust, and in every way they deem feasible seeking to make the execution of that law or policy awkward, expensive, uncomfortable, and (if they can) impossible.

This is civil disobedience in its most extreme form. It sometimes verges on violence. It often requires the use of the protester's own body as a disruptive object, at which point it becomes difficult to determine whether the disobedients are using physical force in their protest. Most serious of all, disobedient resistance deliberately approaches that marginal territory between civil disobedience in the strict sense and rebellion. In one respect the resister is rebelling, openly, against certain uses of authority he deems illegitimate and immoral. To the extent that he defies the law, refusing to recognize even its claim to authority over him, the resister is not practicing civil disobedience at all. Still, most deliberate resistance is undertaken openly, unashamedly, by persons who respect the system of laws as a whole, are generally law-abiding and, by most ordinary standards, are good and honorable citizens. They detest some act or policy, and will not only refuse to cooperate but will disrupt in that sphere. Yet they do not seek the overthrow of the government, or its breakdown. They are neither traitors nor saboteurs. Some critics consider their views revolutionary, and the protesters may use that term in describing themselves, but they are not usually true revolutionaries, for they seek not the dishonor and defeat of their nation but its greater honor and success—through conduct they believe more moral and more in keeping with the ideals their countrymen profess.

It will be seen that resistance presents some knotty theoretical problems. How far must open defiance go before it ceases to be civil disobedience and is rightly considered rebellion? There is no simple answer to this question. So long as the demonstrators' acts meet the basic conditions earlier laid down—are conscientious, public, nonviolent—and so long as they act in such a way as to exhibit their general acceptance of the legitimate authority of government, it is both wise and just to treat them as civil disobedients. In spite of the extremity of their acts, their moral judgments may be sound, and their intensely held and dramatized convictions may serve as a corrective, possibly saving the nation from some gross immorality—perhaps even from catastrophe.

We respect and admire those Germans who, under Hitler's tyranny, risked everything to resist the enforcement of some cruel policies. Many of them were neither rebels nor traitors. They were loyal German citizens, and proud of it. They did not wish to see Germany defeated or humiliated, and they were, on the whole, peaceable and law-abiding. But they could not tolerate some of the gross immoralities in which the German government was then engaged. They would not be complicit. They resisted, in a way requiring great courage and deep moral commitment. We honor them, and wonder why there were not more to stand with them. Now there are those Americans who, only a quarter of a century later,

◆§ *Case 9. The following cases concretely exemplify civil disobedience in the form of resistance.*

(*a*) *A graduate student at The University of Michigan, David Zimmerman, sent the following letter to his local draft board and the local newspaper,* The Michigan Daily (*20 October 1967*), *after taking part in a nationwide return of draft cards to the Selective Service System on 16 October 1967.*

This letter is to inform you that I, as a member of the Resistance, am renouncing the 2-S deferment I have held on your sufferance for the last seven years. I absolutely refuse to cooperate in any way with the Selective Service System. Enclosed is my classification card. I have returned my registration card to the Federal Marshal in New York City.

I refuse to cooperate for the following reasons:

(1) The Selective Service System is grossly unjust. It divides black from white, poor from rich, non-student from student. The 2-S deferment is a class privilege which I can no longer accept.

(2) While you have sent the black and the poor to fight and die you have bought much too cheaply the political emasculation of the white and the well-off. As long as I accept a 2-S deferment I am politically irrelevant to the task of making radical social change in this country. I can no longer permit you to do this to me.

(3) The Selective Service System feeds the manpower require-

honestly believe their government to be acting—within some restricted spheres—in ways equally brutal and immoral. Our government is no Hitlerian tyranny, and any facile equivalence of the two may be rightly denied. But the purity and justice of our international conduct is surely open to question, and there is good evidence that some who act in our name do so with an inhuman disregard for human suffering. If that is true, it is past time to resist—not as rebels, but as loyal Americans deeply concerned for the preservation of our own

ments of the war in Vietnam—a brutal, vicious, immoral war violating the demands of political wisdom, national interest, and common humanity. You insist on cooperating with those who run this war. I will not.

(4) Selective Service is part of a system which aborts attempts in the underdeveloped world to make social revolution. Iran, Guatemala, Cuba, Dominican Republic and Vietnam are a few of the ugliest and most blatant examples. I do not share your paranoid anti-Communism. There are rich nations and there are poor ones. Revolutions will occur in the latter. I refuse to cooperate with your attempts to prevent them.

The Resistance has been formed to organize and encourage non-cooperation with, resistance to, and disruption of the Selective Service System. I am now working with this group.

(b) A Massachusetts organization calling itself Resist in 1967 distributed a statement signed by a considerable number of distinguished American intellectual figures. The complete text of that statement follows.

A CALL TO RESIST ILLEGITIMATE AUTHORITY: TO THE YOUNG MEN OF AMERICA, TO THE WHOLE OF THE AMERICAN PEOPLE, AND TO ALL MEN OF GOODWILL EVERYWHERE:

1. An ever growing number of young American men are finding that the American war in Vietnam so outrages their deepest moral

ideals. If the immorality of our national conduct in these days is later proved—as now seems likely—what will we, who dutifully complied with every government command, say to those who ask: Why did you not resist? Where were the good Americans in those bad days?

Perhaps, in the end, our judgment may be that deliberate resistance by Americans of their lawful government has not been justified by recent events. But even if that be the final verdict, we are wisest and safest to treat those who do so and religious sense that they cannot contribute to it in any way. We share their moral outrage.

2. We further believe that the war is unconstitutional and illegal. Congress has not declared a war as required by the Constitution. Moreover, under the Constitution, treaties signed by the President and ratified by the Senate have the same force as the Constitution itself. The Charter of the United Nations is such a treaty. The Charter specifically obligates the United States to refrain from force or the threat of force in international relations. It requires member states to exhaust every peaceful means of settling disputes and to submit disputes which cannot be settled peacefully to the Security Council. The United States has systematically violated all of these Charter provisions for thirteen years.

3. Moreover, this war violates international agreements, treaties, and principles of law which the United States Government has solemnly endorsed. The combat role of the United States troops in Vietnam violates the Geneva Accords of 1954 which our government pledged to support but has since subverted. The destruction of rice, crops, and livestock; the burning and bulldozing of entire villages consisting exclusively of civilian structures; the interning of civilian non-combatants in concentration camps; the summary executions of civilians in captured villages who could not produce satisfactory evidence of their loyalties or did not wish

resist as civil disobedients, and not as revolutionaries, so long as they will permit us to do so. Their resistance will not shake the security of the nation, nor seriously interfere with its life and well-being. It may, if we are sensitive, cause us to act with more reflection and greater restraint. As a purely theoretical problem, there is no clear answer to the question of whether those who openly resist the law are civil disobedients or simply misguided rebels. But as a practical problem in determining the most reasonable course, it is clear to be removed to concentration camps; the slaughter of peasants who dared to stand up in their fields and shake their fists at American helicopters—these are all actions of the kind which the United States and the other victorious powers of World War II declared to be crimes against humanity for which individuals are responsible even when acting under the orders of their governments and for which Germans were sentenced at Nuremberg to long prison terms and death. The prohibition of such acts as war crimes was incorporated in treaty law by the Geneva Conventions of 1949, ratified by the United States. These are commitments to other countries and to Mankind, and they would claim our allegiance even if Congress should declare war.

4. We also believe it is an unconstitutional denial of religious liberty and equal protection of the laws to withhold draft exemption from men whose religious or profound philosophical beliefs are opposed to what in the Western religious tradition have been long known as unjust wars.

5. Therefore, we believe on all these grounds that every free man has a legal right and a moral duty to exert every effort to end this war, to avoid collusion with it, and to encourage others to do the same. Young men in the armed forces or threatened with the draft face the most excruciating choices. For them various forms of resistance risk separation from their families and their country, destruction of their careers, loss of their freedom,

that resistance should be viewed as one form—albeit an extreme one—of civil disobedience. (See Case 9.)

Finally, having distinguished direct from indirect civil disobedience, and moral from political civil disobedience, it is well to point out that the two pairs of categories do often but not always coincide. Moral civil disobedience is almost always direct. Principles governing a personal conscience are likely to oblige disobedience only of laws that offend those principles—not of any law that may effectively serve some and loss of their lives. Each must choose the course of resistance dictated by his conscience and circumstances. Among those already in the armed forces some are refusing to obey specific illegal and immoral orders, some are attempting to educate their fellow servicemen on the murderous and barbarous nature of the war, some are absenting themselves without official leave. Among those not in the armed forces some are applying for status as conscientious objectors to American aggression in Vietnam, some are refusing to be inducted. Among both groups some are resisting openly and paying a heavy penalty, some are organizing more resistance within the United States, and some have sought sanctuary in other countries.

6. We believe that each of these forms of resistance against illegitimate authority is courageous and justified. Many of us believe that open resistance to the war and the draft is the course of action most likely to strengthen the moral resolve with which all of us can oppose the war and most likely to bring an end to the war.

7. We will continue to lend our support to those who undertake resistance to this war. We will raise funds to organize draft resistance unions, to supply legal defense and bail, to support families, and otherwise aid resistance to the war in whatever ways may seem appropriate.

8. We firmly believe that our statement is the sort of speech that under the First Amendment must be free, and that the actions we will undertake are as legal as is the war resistance of

strategic purpose. But moral disobedience is not invariably direct. When the object of the protest is a policy not within the power of a protester to disobey directly, he may, out of moral compunction chiefly, disobey some other law that will exhibit his ethical stand. This precisely is the position of many who, when their government engages in a war they believe unjust, refuse to pay a portion of their taxes. It is the young men themselves. In any case we feel that we cannot shrink from fulfilling our responsibilities to the youth whom many of us teach, to the country whose freedom we cherish, and to the ancient traditions of religion and philosophy which we strive to preserve in this generation.

9. We call upon all men of good will to join us in this confrontation with immoral authority. Especially we call upon the universities to fulfill their mission of enlightenment and religious organizations to honor their heritage of brotherhood. Now is the time to resist.

(c) *Planning to destroy their draft cards publicly, as an act of protest against American military involvement in Vietnam, in March 1967 a group of young men in Ithaca, New York, distributed an open plea for support, which read in part:*

Body and soul, we are oppressed in common. Body and soul, we must resist in common. The undersigned believe that we should [support] this mass resistance by publicly destroying our draft cards at the Spring Mobilization. . . . We urge all people who have contemplated the act of destroying their draft cards to carry out this act on April 15, with the understanding that this pledge becomes binding only when 500 people have made it. . . . We are ready to put ourselves on the line for this position. . . . We are fully aware that our action makes us liable for penalties of up to five years in prison and $10,000 in fines. . . . ᘒ

not the tax laws to which they object but the immoral uses to which the levied funds are put. Neither do they suppose that their refusal will have much influence on government policy. Yet they feel obliged to make their moral stand concrete, engaging in a course of action that is chiefly detrimental to themselves. (See Case 10.)

Politically motivated disobedience may be direct or indi-

◄§ *Case 10. Indirect moral disobedience is illustrated by the following concrete examples.*

(a) In the spring of 1967 an open letter was distributed nationally by the No Tax for War Committee, of Cincinnati, Ohio. Signed by scholars from all over the country, the letter read in part:

By April 15th, every American citizen must decide whether he will make a voluntary contribution to the continuation of this war. After grave consideration we have decided that we can no longer do so, and that we will therefore withhold all or part of the taxes due. The purpose of this letter is to call your attention to the fact that a nationwide tax refusal campaign is in progress, as stated in the accompanying announcement, and to urge you to consider refusing to contribute voluntarily to this barbaric war.

Accompanying this letter was a statement for which signatures were invited, reading, "Because so much of the tax paid the federal government goes for poisoning of food crops, blasting of villages, napalming and killing of thousands upon thousands of people, as in Vietnam at the present time, I am not going to pay taxes on 1966 income."

(b) An Associated Press dispatch of 27 March 1967, appearing in the Ann Arbor News, read in part:

rect. The politically motivated protester will, of course, choose to violate those laws that he concludes will give his protest its greatest effectiveness. To that end trespass laws and the like are often carefully chosen. But in some circumstances the protester may conclude that greatest political effectiveness will be achieved by disobedience of the law that is itself the object of protest—as in breaking segregation statutes or induction laws. In short, moral disobedience is usually direct, and political disobedience is usually indirect; but moral dis-

Detroit: Nearly 40 Michigan Quakers defied the federal government Sunday as they gave $1,400 to Canadian Quakers to buy medical supplies for North Vietnam. The money was presented to the Canadian Friends Service Committee at a Detroit home. Later the Michigan Quakers marched across the Ambassador Bridge—linking Detroit and Windsor, Ontario—and gave the Canadians a Bible containing a symbolic 1-dollar bill. The Bible was open to the passage: "If your enemy is hungry, feed him. If he is thirsty, give him drink."

The Treasury Department had warned that the donation would be a violation of the Trading with the Enemy Act and the Export Control Act. A leader of the Michigan Quakers, Gilbert S. Hamilton, Dearborn, said the Treasury Department had refused permission for the donation in January on grounds that distribution of the medical supplies among North Vietnamese could not be supervised. . . .   .

Meanwhile, in Buffalo, N.Y., some 300 pacifists, mostly Quakers, crossed the Peace Bridge into Canada Sunday bearing some $100 worth of medical supplies for shipment to North and South Vietnam. Conviction under the acts cited by the Treasury Department could result in 10-year prison terms and $10,000 fines. ঽ

obedience may be indirect at times, and political disobedience is often direct. These two sets of categories—the one focused chiefly on the act, the other on the actor—provide different and separable perspectives from which instances of civil disobedience may be approached.

⊸ः IV ॐ

THE PUNISHMENT OF
CIVIL DISOBEDIENCE

1. CIVIL DISOBEDIENCE SHOULD BE PUNISHED

One who deliberately breaks the law should be punished for that conduct. The civil disobedient deliberately breaks a law he knows applies to him, and he is no exception to the rule. He is properly subject to the normal punishment for the offense he commits.

What is this offense? And why is one normally punished for committing that offense? Answers to these questions will render the entire issue of punishment in such cases much clearer.

The first question is easily answered. It is some element in the criminal law that the civil disobedient disobeys. By definition, he commits some crime, although it is likely to be a very minor one. However, it is not "civil disobedience" that is his crime; as noted earlier, there is no such crime. He is guilty of an infraction of some particular law—of doing something the law forbids, or refusing to do something the law commands. The determination of appropriate punishment in every case, therefore, depends upon the character and gravity of the particular criminal offense of which he is found guilty. A punishment standard for all civil disobedients is clearly out of the question.

Once the guilt of the disobedient has been formally established, the precise punishment to be imposed depends largely, in the American legal system, upon the judge of the trial court. Within limits established by the statute, the court usually has wide discretionary powers in fixing sentence. The intelligent use of these discretionary powers is rightly left to the good judgment of the magistrate. Some observations concerning the use of these discretionary powers, however, are in order.

2. THE GROUNDS AND SEVERITY OF PUNISHMENT

Three possible objectives traditionally have been distinguished as the chief aims of the punishments provided by criminal law. The first is *deterrence*—keeping the offender from acting similarly in the future, and, by example, causing others who might be tempted to refrain from committing that offense. "This law means business," the punishing authority says in effect. "He who violates it will be fined or imprisoned in such-and-such a way. This clearly applies now to you who have already broken this law. Let your punishment serve as public notice to all potential future violators of it that they must not expect to avoid the same treatment." Many of the punishments inflicted by parents on their children, by teachers on their students, and by courts on criminal offenders, are based chiefly (and sometimes solely) on this deterrence theory. In some cases it is a bad theory. Punishments, even when certain to follow the offense, do not effectively deter some offenders from some kinds of forbidden activity. But deterrence is effective in many situations. The rigorous enforcement of traffic laws, for example, may not be the best assurance of highway safety, but it is one very useful device for maintaining a degree of good order and reasonable sanity on the roads. Many are they who would occasionally or frequently disregard traffic regulations were it not for the deterring threat of punishment if caught.

A second objective of law enforcement through punishment is *reform*. The criminal being one who has broken the rules by which society lives, he must be caused to see the gravity of his offense. He must be punished (if that is the right word) or treated in such a manner as to create in him a respect for the law, and a desire and ability to live within it in reasonable harmony with fellow citizens. Punishment is here conceived as a device to develop or reinforce an accord between the internal motivations of the offender and the external demands of law and order. "We seek to instruct you, and to rehabilitate you," say the punishing officers to the offender, in effect, "not merely to visit you with pain, or to make good our threats. For your own sake, and that of your society, you must be changed. That change is the aim of what we now do to you." Most courts and penal systems profess some such goal as their highest objective, but in practice the punishments commonly meted out are not consistent with that stated intention. Most fines and jail sentences —by far the most common forms of punishment—do little to effect the internal reform of the offender. There is overwhelming evidence to show, in fact, that prisons especially are a contributing cause of hardened criminality, and that they promote rather than prevent lives of habitual lawlessness. The reform theory of punishment is enlightened and humane. But it clearly cannot be the sole or even the prime justification for most actual legal punishments, and very likely it could not suffice, even in a more nearly ideal society, to explain why law-breakers should be punished.

A third theory upon which punishment is often based is that of *retribution*. It is right and fitting, according to this view, that the wrongdoer be visited with some evil proportionate to his crime. "An eye for an eye and a tooth for a tooth" seemed a suitable principle in more primitive times; retribution has now become far more sophisticated. Finding the appropriate penalty may be difficult in many cases, but the effort goes on.

> My object all sublime
> I shall achieve in time—
> To make the punishment fit the crime,
> The punishment fit the crime.

So sings Gilbert and Sullivan's Mikado, and his goal is the essential goal of every modern penal system, according to this retributive theory. Hence, very serious crimes are punished with long prison terms; less serious crimes with shorter sentences or fines alone. The point is not that a twenty-year sentence will deter twice as effectively as a ten-year sentence, or that it will reform twice as well. Probably it will do neither. Yet some crimes seem to *deserve* heavier sentences than others. It is not what the punishment may accomplish in the future, for those convicted or for other persons, but how suitable it is in view of past acts that determines its justice. "The legal wrong you have committed," says the law to the offender, "being of a certain kind, calls for your punishment in a certain degree. It is to be hoped that you will reform your ways, and that you and others will be at least deterred from offending so in the future, but however that may be the punishment now meted out to you is your just desert." Retributive theories of punishment have often been attacked as being primitive, cruel, and unenlightened, exhibiting a spirit of vengeance not becoming in civilized men. There is truth in these criticisms; yet there is truth, too, in the claim that our practice of punishing (in enforcing the law, and in other less formal circumstances) almost invariably incorporates some retributive element. We seek the punishment that is not only *effective* (in deterring or reforming) but *just*, and we often seem to suppose that its justice is a matter at least partly separable from its consequences. Retribution by itself is no satisfactory guide to appropriate legal punishment; but no system of punishment is likely to be complete without recognizing some retributive elements.

These three theories of punishment—deterrence, reform, and retribution—have been much discussed and refined by philosophers and penologists. Probably it is not one of them alone, but some mixture of two or the three, that will provide the best theoretical ground for legal punishment. In determining the appropriate penalty for particular concrete cases the punishing authority is usually obliged to use considerable discretionary powers. Making the best use of those powers requires a clear understanding of the aims of punishment in cases of the kind in question. Only with some end in view can a sentence be imposed that is most likely to achieve that end.

This is especially true for civil disobedients, because they are not run-of-the-mill outlaws. Rather, they break the law under special circumstances and in special states of mind.

The severity of punishment meted out to them, therefore, will be very largely dependent upon the aims of the authorities, upon the theory of punishment chiefly relied upon by the sentencing magistrate.

If the magistrate views punishment as basically retributive, he is likely to impose upon the civil disobedient a near maximum penalty for the specific offense committed—say, trespass. For, he will argue, this offender's act was much worse than that of most trespassers. Not only did he do what the law forbade, but he did so with full knowledge that he was committing a crime, and with the deliberate intention and desire to commit that crime. His aim was not merely to do a particular thing but to break the law in doing it. His offense, therefore, when fully understood, is as bad as it can be under this statute. He did the wrongful deed, *and* did it with a spirit of deliberate defiance and lawlessness that, if generally acted out, would undermine a society. That precisely is what the law deems most culpable, and must therefore punish most severely.

This line of reasoning has been most commonly adopted by judges before whom civil disobedients have been tried. Their reaction has frequently been one of irritation and anger. The sentence they impose has often been accompanied by a lecture sternly reprimanding the protester for the willful disobedience that has been freely admitted. And often they have inflicted punishment with all or almost all of the severity their discretionary powers would permit.

Some trial judges have gone to the other extreme. Conscious of the deep ethical commitments of the civil disobedients before them, and very possibly sharing the moral ideals those disobedients sought to further, they have imposed punishments at or near the minimum permitted by the law in question. An infraction of the statute has been established, such judges reason, and punishment must be given. But if the ultimate object of the law is to encourage citizens to build a peaceful and harmonious society in which one's fellows are respected and principles of justice manifested, there is no need to punish these civil disobedients severely. They are already of that mind. Consistency requires some punishment; human decency and an understanding of the correct reasons for punishment requires that it be, in such cases, as light as can be. Here the underlying theory of punishment is reform. The aim of law enforcement is supposed (explicitly or implicitly) to be the development and reinforcement of wholesome social habits and attitudes. If the civil disobedient—his single infraction to the contrary notwithstanding—is known to have the desired attitudes and habits; if the testimony of his associates and teachers establishes the high integrity of his character, and the record of his past conduct establishes his understanding and support of good social practices; and if in the judge's own estimation the morality and intelligence of the disobedient are high, perhaps much higher than the average of persons appearing before that court, it would be quite unreasonable, he might conclude, to impose any sentence beyond the minimum. It would be appropriate, in sentencing, to remind the disobedient firmly of the seriousness of his deliberate violation of law; and it might even be appropriate to add an appreciation of the moral integrity which led to that violation.

An intermediate course might well be followed by a magistrate whose prime concern in fixing punishment is deterrence. The disobedient has, without lawful excuse, committed an act the statute specifically forbids. The same statute provides that punishment be imposed (within certain limits), and it does so with the pretty clear intention that all persons be thus warned of the consequences of a disregard for that law. Now this civil disobedient, such a magistrate may reason, is clearly one of those to whom that law refers. It is a straightforward and simple statute and makes no reference either to the spirit of defiance or the nobility of character of the violator. Such matters do not bear upon the guilt for, or the punishment of, the crime he has committed. It is an essential element in the just execution of all laws that every person found guilty of violating them be treated alike (or as nearly so as possible) provided their record of past infractions is also like. Now it has been the long-standing practice of this court (his reasoning may continue) to impose upon persons found guilty of this crime, who have no record of earlier convictions, a sentence of x days in jail, and a fine of y dollars, suspending both (or the jail sentence only) when it is a first offense. There is no good reason within the purview of the court on this occasion to treat this civil disobedient any differently. The aim of this punishment being to deter this and other potential offenders from future like offenses, it is important that this threat not be weakened by letting off lightly those whom the court may happen to admire. By the same token it is unreasonable to impose special severity upon those of whom the court happens to disapprove. The issue is solely one of the infraction of this (trespass or other) statute, not of the motivating spirit of that infraction. For such infractions, under circumstances like these, effective deterrence requires consistent punishment for all, civil disobedients included.

Thus the three theories of punishment, whether explicitly or implicitly held, are likely (but not certain, of course) to lead to different decisions in practice.

A fourth analysis, wisest of all, is also likely to lead to the intermediate result supported by the deterrence theory alone. According to this analysis, the magistrate may suppose that the ground for punishment lies not in retribution or reform or deterrence taken singly, but in some complicated mixture of the three. Unlike the pure deterrence analysis above, such a magistrate may reason that, in fixing sentence within the discretionary limits set for him, it is not only possible but obligatory for him to inquire into the spirit with which the law was broken and the moral objectives of the disobedient act. These factors are irrelevant, he may allow, in determining the guilt of the accused. But once guilt is established, they are highly relevant factors in deciding upon appropriate punishment. Guilt is for the crime alone, and looks narrowly at the act. Punishment is of the criminal, and looks widely at the actor as well as at his act. Having genuinely intended to do just what he did, and knowing that act was a violation of a duly enacted statute, the noblest motives in the world will not expunge his guilt; nor would a spirit of willful defiance create any legal guilt had the law not been broken in deed. The law having been broken, however, the task becomes that of setting the most appropriate punishment (given the complex goals of punishment) for that specific person, under the specific circumstances of his time and place. The attitudes he adopts toward the arresting officer, the court, and the laws in general tell much about him and how he might be most appropriately treated. That he breaks the law knowingly, and perhaps with a defiant spirit, does not speak well for him, although much the same description can be given of many offenders against the same laws who are not civil disobedients. But if the deliberateness of his act may weigh against him, it must be registered in his favor that his act was not done out of self-serving interests but (however misguided it may have been) with honorable motives and out of real concern for the welfare of the whole society. The absence of selfishness, the candor, the moral integrity that the civil disobedient is likely to manifest, all should serve at least to balance any tendency toward increased severity of treatment. In the end, a wise judge may conclude, the factors possibly calling for special treatment approximately cancel each other out. And since deterrence is likely to be a major objective of punishments imposed under the criminal laws, and both that deterrent effect and fairness in view of the circumstances are best achieved by consistent punishment for such infractions, the most just punishment for a civil disobedient, all things considered, is the same punishment that would normally be set for an ordinary infraction of the same law. Principles of consistency and equal treatment are thereby honored, the charge of partiality toward or prejudice against the civil disobedient is forestalled, and the legal system as a whole is protected from abuse.

In short, it would not be unreasonable, in determining proper punishment, to treat a case of civil disobedience simply as an infraction, without attending to its special circumstances. If, however, its circumstances are to affect the punishment, all circumstances, those in the protester's favor as well as those not, should be weighed. Results of the two procedures are likely to be substantially the same.

One qualification needs to be added for cases of direct

civil disobedience in which the legal offense is grave. In such cases—for example, deliberate refusal to report for induction into military service—the fixing of punishment is a most serious and delicate matter. The fact that the disobedient act was done openly and out of conscience might, in these cases, reasonably be given some weight in mitigating punishment. "Evasion of the draft" might be the crime of which the disobedient is technically convicted, but his act, although criminal, is likely to have been in no way evasive or clandestine. Similarly in other acts of direct, moral disobedience, the good character of the man, and the reformatory aim of the laws, may play a very considerable role in determining punishment. The deterrence of others who are not civil disobedients from breaking that law may require that the civil disobedient be punished; but nothing is gained, in such cases, by imposing more than the minimal punishment the law permits. Extralong prison terms will not make better men of these disobedients, nor much deter others of similar conviction. Severe punishment, however, may hinder the contribution those persons can make to society, and it is quite likely to further enrage and embitter them. If a man's conscience forbids him to comply with what he deeply believes to be an unjust law, that conflict does not excuse him from compliance or from punishment for disobedience. But the response of the community to such a man will be an index of its sophistication and humaneness.

3. THE ROLE OF PUNISHMENT
IN DISOBEDIENT PROTEST

The civil disobedient fully understands that his unlawful act is properly subject to legal punishment. Being, like most men, fond of his freedom, the prospect of arrest and punishment cannot please him and is likely to frighten him. He must recognize, nevertheless, that such punishment is an unavoidable consequence of the protest he has chosen to make.

Most civil disobedients have no doubt in their own minds, and make no issue in court, over their legal guilt. Their disobedience was deliberate and knowing. They expect to be arrested and charged with a crime. Normally they intend from the outset to plead guilty to that charge if it is accurate. In some cases, believing their act to be morally right although legally wrong, they may, rather than admitting guilt, plead no contest (*nolo contendere*), which has essentially the same result as a guilty plea. In any event, they expect to be found guilty of a crime (usually a very minor one) and expect to be punished for it by fine or prison sentence or both.

This legal punishment is more than a possible outcome of the disobedient's act—it is the natural and proper culmination of it. His disobedient act is essentially one of protest, but it is protest within a framework of laws whose legitimacy he accepts. His submission to public punishment is therefore essential. It is vital in exhibiting his intense personal concern over the issue at hand. It gives concrete proof of his deep commitment to the cause for which he protests. He demonstrates thereby his willingness even to sacrifice himself in behalf of that cause.

As a tactical matter, as well as one of principle, the disobedient may welcome punishment, while personally dreading it. Arrest and trial and conviction all are likely to catch the public eye, especially if the protester be one of respected position in the community. The reason for his disobedience —the wrong he hopes to help correct—will be appearing repeatedly in news reports and commentary as a result of this punishment. Even refusing the option of a fine and deliberately going to jail for five or ten days, or more, may be one way to increase the publicity of his protest and, if his community is morally sensitive, to increase its effectiveness as well.

For similar reasons it generally will be inappropriate for him to seek acquittal of the crime he deliberately committed. Knowing that his act was a violation of law, he must realize that legal punishment cannot be bypassed, or the infraction excused, because of the noble (or at least subjectively conscientious) motivation of his protest. Indeed, it is just because it is a crime, and known by actor and public to be punishable, that the act is chosen and serves as a dramatic form of protest. It is inconsistent, therefore, with the whole spirit of his enterprise for the civil disobedient, having deliberately disobeyed the law in protest, to seek to be let off from punishment because his motives were good. He would be foolish to expect that result and wrong to pursue it.

Moreover, it is tactically unwise, in view of the protester's own objectives, for him to seek acquittal. The effectiveness of his protest is largely a result of the impression made upon an apathetic public by a zealous and devoted minority. Because he suffers the unpleasant consequences of his disobedience, and does so willingly, his act has a moral impact, and that impact is vital to whatever success he hopes for. So soon as any effort is begun to escape those consequences, the self-sacrificial element in the protest is publicly dissipated, the moral impact much reduced. Were the civil disobedient to seek acquittal of the crime he did in fact commit, a skeptical public would be reinforced in doubt. Freed from the need to ponder the reasons for the disobedience, they will grasp quickly at the now plausible explanation that it was sheer defiance mixed with self-interest that lay behind the act. By giving apparent support to that claim, any civil disobedient who pleads not guilty undermines whatever beneficial effects his own and allied protests might produce. (See Chapter VI, Section 2.)

Some argue, in opposition to the view here expressed, that the civil disobedient ought not accept punishment for his act, because such acceptance gives support to an unjust legal system. Professor Howard Zinn has been the most forceful advocate of this latter view. It is a fallacy, he contends, to suppose that

a person who commits civil disobedience must accept his punishment as right. . . . Why must the citizen "accept the result" of a decision he considers immoral? To support "the rule of law" in the abstract? . . . To support a wrong rule of law does not automatically strengthen the right rule of law, indeed may weaken it. . . . The sportsmanlike acceptance of jail as the terminus of civil disobedience is fine for a football game, or for a society determined to limit reform to tokens. It does not suit a society which wants to eliminate long-festering wrongs. [Howard Zinn, Disobedience and Democracy, Random House, New York, 1968, pp. 27, 31.]

Zinn's argument comes to this: if a law is grossly unjust, any punishment for deliberately breaking it is unjust, and therefore the disobedient need not accept any such punishment administered by the state.

The argument has some plausibility, but its conclusion is partly wrong, and the mistake is a consequence of an insufficiently refined analysis. The matter is complicated; Zinn and others try to make it appear simple.

Whether a civil disobedient ought to "accept his punishment as right" depends upon what he did, what kind of law he broke, and under what circumstances. The distinction between direct and indirect civil disobedience, emphasized earlier (see Chapter III, Section 2), is an important factor in determining the "rightness" of punishment. If the disobedience was direct, the protester deliberately disobeying a law he honestly thought immoral in itself, he is justified, of course, in fighting punishment in every reasonable way at his command, chiefly through the courts. He will seek to have the bad law struck down, or at least to have it declared inapplicable in his case. If he loses in the end, he is likely, as a citizen who is generally law-abiding, to accept the punishment, not as *right* but as a painful price he pays to help maintain a law-governed community. If the law he broke really was in itself immoral (and we may be in some doubt about that), the legal system will have done an injustice in punishing him; but no system can allow every man to sit as the judge in his own case. Of course justice is not always done, and the battle against bad laws must never stop; but miscarriages of justice do not, in themselves, justify the abandonment of a legal system, or the abandonment of normal procedures whenever one accused under them complains of injustice.

If, on the other hand, the disobedience has been indirect, the disobedient having broken what he knows to be itself a good law (a traffic or trespass law, or the like) to protest some other evil (say, the testing of nuclear weapons), it is right for him to be punished, not because he is a bad man but because, as I argued above, liability to punishment in cases of indirect disobedience is an essential part of the act of protest itself. If indirect civil disobedience is to be an effective tactic, it must do much more than disrupt; it must exhibit the depth and intensity of the commitment of the protester. To be a successful political act within the system, it must be a genuinely moral act within that system. It cannot be such if the system is disregarded or despised. The beauty of this kind of protest lies in the fact that, although the law is broken, the system of laws is respected. (See Chapter II, Section 3.) Accepting the punishment, when one has deliberately broken a good law, is the only way to show this respect convincingly. To evade punishment in such cases, therefore, is to emasculate the protest.

❧ V ☙

THE JUSTIFICATION OF
CIVIL DISOBEDIENCE

1. RECOGNITION, JUSTIFICATION, AND GENERALIZATION

It is one thing to identify an act as a clear case of civil disobedience and another thing entirely to judge its rightness. The former requires criteria of recognition, with which I have been largely concerned up to this point; the latter requires criteria of justification, with which I shall be largely concerned from this point on. An act is justifiable if a reasoned demonstration of its rightness can be given. Because there is much uncertainty and disagreement over what is meant by rightness, and how it can be established, there is bound to be uncertainty and disagreement also over claims that acts of civil disobedience are justified or unjustified. Such issues cannot be resolved simply or beyond controversy; they will remain perennially subjects of philosophical and political dispute. Careful reflection, however, while not ending such disputes, may clarify what is at issue, and may provide a rational framework within which argument can continue intelligibly and profitably. It may also be possible to reach some larger conclusions about how the defense (or criticism) of civil disobedience might most reasonably be carried on.

The construction of this rational framework is the aim of what follows. From the outset I disclaim any effort to show that civil disobedience, taken generally, is always justified, or is never justified. Both of these extreme views are almost certainly false. Recognizing how various are the laws the disobedient may break, how different may be the objects of his protest, and how complicated and variable may be the contexts in which the disobedience takes place, we must be very cautious indeed in affirming conclusions about all cases of civil disobedience, and very loathe to say that all of it, or none of it, is justified. What may prove justifiable, or unjustifiable, after careful analysis, is not civil disobedience *überhaupt*, but this or that act of civil disobedience in a given and well-understood social context. Only in the light of these contextual considerations can specific acts of protest be fairly judged.

In spite of the variety of contexts, however, we can reach some general conclusions about the paths that reasoned justification may or may not follow. These conclusions will not enable one to say, flatly, whether a given act of civil disobedience is right, or wrong; but they will help one to undertake the rational appraisal that the particular act of civil disobedience probably requires and deserves.

Throughout, the distinction earlier drawn between civil disobedience and revolution (see Chapter II, Section 3), should be kept in mind. What may serve to justify a rebellion may very likely justify unlawful protest also, but the converse is not true. The civil disobedient does not seek to overthrow the Constitution, or the system of laws, and we must be careful not to impose upon him the far weightier task of the kind of justification that we rightly demand from the revolutionary. In both cases, however, deep questions regarding the limits of the obligations owed by a citizen to his state are being raised. Civil disobedience must be sharply differentiated from revolution but is, like it, a very serious matter.

2. CIVIL DISOBEDIENCE AND LEGAL JUSTIFICATION

It follows from the nature of an act of civil disobedience that it cannot be given a legal justification. Within a given juridical system, the law cannot justify the violation of the law. Often, it is true, laws conflict, or appear to do so. Such conflicts are ultimately resolved by determining which of the conflicting elements is controlling in the given case. Making that determination may require the invocation of some higher principle not yet explicitly expressed in the legal system. However wisely, some resolution of the conflict of laws is likely to be achieved, and the statute or common law principle overruled in that resolution is no longer, to that extent or in that context, the law. The law may justify an act, but it cannot justify an unlawful act.

A familiar illustration is the case of the motorist who, stopping at a red traffic signal, is directed by a policeman to drive through that signal. He faces no serious dilemma. It is the law that one must not drive through red lights. But it is also the law that one must obey the instructions of authorized police officers, and traffic ordinances usually make it very clear that in cases of conflict the instructions of the officer take precedence, for it is as their instruments that mechanical signals are employed. The motorist in that situation must drive through the red light, of course. In doing so he does not break the law. Conflicts within the legal system are rarely that simple; but, however complex, their resolutions always seek, as in this easy case, to maintain or reestablish the consistency of the hierarchy of laws, so that an act, once clearly described, either is or is not an offense within that system.

Such consistency is not always realized in fact. Often a citizen, with the best of intentions and legal counsel, may be genuinely uncertain, in view of an apparent inconsistency in the legal system, whether an act he contemplates is lawful; he may be unable to determine beforehand how that legal conflict will be ultimately resolved. These uncertainties are surely regrettable, but they cannot be said to justify an act that is ultimately pronounced illegal. In the light of his unavoidable quandary, such a person may escape punishment; but if his act is held unlawful at last, there is no way in which the laws of that system can justify it.

Sometimes a specific law may open clearly restricted legal avenues to those whose conscience or religion forbids their compliance with its major commands. Outstanding examples of this are the careful provisions often made for conscientious objectors to required military service. But those who use these provisions do not disobey any law; they are, on the contrary, meticulously law-abiding. What is legally justified by such provisions is a particular course of action, given some carefully specified qualifications; they never justify, nor could they justify, deliberate disobedience. (See Chapter II, Section 2.)

Are there no exceptions to the principle that civil disobedience cannot be legally justified? A careful examination of cases sometimes claimed to be exceptions will show that there are none.

It sometimes happens that a citizen will believe, in good

faith, that a certain law deprives him of some constitutionally guaranteed right and is therefore invalid. His belief may be correct or incorrect, but to determine this the issue must be brought before the courts, whose job it is, in the American system, to judge the constitutionality of legislation. Normally, one cannot simply ask some court to rule on this matter but must bring the statute to judicial test. Such a challenge is usually possible only through an actual case, in which the right in question is exercised through an infraction of the statute that is the object of attack. This infraction is likely to be deliberate and carefully thought out in advance. It aims at the ultimate nullification of a specific law and at least seeks to compel some clarification of its constitutional status. Some might argue that since this clarification is highly desirable for all, and since it can come only as a result of a challenge through infraction, the deliberate disobedience of law that initiates such a challenge is justified by that legal system. The legal system, then, appears to justify some cases of civil disobedience.

This conclusion is not correct. It is the result of a confusion between what the structure of the system may encourage and what the laws of the system may justify. The claim of justifiability derives its plausibility from the fact that the peculiarities of our legal system may make deliberate violation of a law a convenient instrument of attack upon it. But no legal system can be said to *justify* all conduct that seeks to challenge one of its elements, and certainly it cannot justify challenge in the form of disobedience. Such challenge must go forward at the risk of the challenger. If he is not prepared to take that risk he must rely upon the channels of legislative amendment or repeal. If he does challenge the law by deliberately violating it, and the law is ultimately held to be constitutional and valid, he must expect to pay not only the costs of the judicial test but the penalty of the original disobedience as well. Part of his aim may have been the laudable one of legal clarification. But if the act through which the clarification is sought is found, in the end, to have been unlawful, that laudable objective cannot be said to give the act legal justification.

Much may be said about the advantages and disadvantages of a legal system so organized as to permit the testing of the constitutionality of laws only through litigation on specific infractions. It is an inconvenient system for one who believes his rights infringed by some statute. It is, on the other hand, a system that greatly encourages restraint by the courts (who are not, after all, the originators of the laws nor usually the direct representatives of the people) and obliges them to restrict the applicability of their pronouncements to concrete cases in which the factual context is given, and to other situations essentially similar. This is a real hindrance to constitutional testing and a limitation upon the power of judges. But it has not generally prevented judicial remedy for crass violations of constitutional right; and it is probably a desirable restriction where the law-making power of the government is vested fundamentally in a legislature consisting of the people's elected representatives. In any event, that is the character of the American legal system. Fully understood, its structure cannot be held to justify disobedience of law.

It may happen that such a challenge to the constitutionality of a law will prove successful—that the law in question will be declared unconstitutional by the highest court, and hence invalid. After such a finding the act of the challenger,

originally appearing to be deliberate lawlessness, is justified
and his prosecution quashed. Are not such cases instances of
legal justification of civil disobedience? Surely not. What has
been found lawful in such cases is the act of the challenger,
and the court may do this by striking down (or otherwise
invalidating for the case at hand) the statute he was charged
with disobeying. The upshot of such proceedings is the estab-
lishment of the innocence of his conduct. But if the conduct
was legally innocent there was not, after all, any genuine legal
disobedience. The law defied proved to be not a good law at
all, or proved to be inapplicable in cases of just that kind. Successful challenge in the courts cannot yield legal justification
of civil disobedience, because the fact of success cancels the
legal infraction that is an essential element of civil disobedience.

Deliberate challenge of a law believed unconstitutional is
often not successful. When the ultimate finding of the courts
upholds the law under attack the original conduct is indeed a
violation of law. The disobedience may have been (although
it need not be) deliberate—but the legal result provides no
justification of it. Again, the law cannot justify the breaking
of the law within a given legal system.

In some cases the challenge presented by apparent disobedience may not be directed at the validity of the statute but
at the validity of its application in certain ways or under certain circumstances. Laws valid on their face may be improperly applied so as to defeat constitutionally protected rights.
No one will deny, for example, the right of a community to
enact legislation that prohibits littering and penalizes it by
heavy fine. The use of such laws to prevent the distribution

of political pamphlets, however, will rightly be held an unconstitutional application of them. Again, it may be entirely reasonable to require that the organization of a parade through city streets first be cleared with municipal officials to insure that there is preparation for the consequent disruption of traffic and that the inconvenience of nonparticipants is minimized. But using such licensing powers to prohibit parades because they support political views unpopular with the city administration will be found unconstitutional. In such cases the applications of the statutes are invalidated while the laws themselves may be allowed to stand. The logical status of the justificatory procedure is the same in these situations as when statutes are altogether struck down. Ultimate legal justification of the challenger's conduct nullifies any finding of disobedience; ultimate legal finding of disobedience nullifies any claim to legal justification.

All this is very well in theory, it may be replied, but we seem to have obscured, with words, many of the actual cases of what is commonly called civil disobedience. For that expression is often used to describe the act of one who deliberately breaks a local ordinance in the honest belief that it could not stand the test of higher judicial scrutiny. Suppose (as is often the case) that he is correct in that belief. He may not have the time, or the money, or the ability to pursue his rights in court. Pressing an appeal through the courts, on constitutional principles, requires considerable financial backing and extraordinary patience. Even if one is fully prepared for this ordeal, he is likely to be tried and convicted by local authorities, and may even be punished (perhaps harshly) if he is not quick and clever in seeking judicial relief during appeal.

And the appeal, though right in principle, may fail on some procedural technicality. In short, even when the statute does infringe on constitutionally protected rights, an ultimate legal justification of the rightful act that violates that wrongful statute is only rarely forthcoming. In such cases the infraction and its punishment are indeed present. Yet (by hypothesis) we agree the act is ultimately justifiable before the law. Shall we then say that this is not civil disobedience? Or should we say that it is civil disobedience, but legally justifiable?

The puzzle presented here arises out of conflicts between principles at different levels of authority. The hierarchy of authorities is a practical necessity in a large state and a logical necessity in a federal system such as that of the United States. The citizen is properly subject to local, *and* state, *and* national laws. Within certain spheres municipal and state laws suffice; where constitutional issues, foreign affairs, or various other special matters enter, federal law is supreme. The several systems of law—municipal, county, state, national—are concomitant and are for the most part consistent. When inconsistencies arise (or are claimed to arise), only complicated litigation can fully resolve the matter.

Whether we say of the case described above (an act in deliberate violation of local statute but really protected by constitutional guarantees) that it is or is not civil disobedience, or that it is or is not legally justifiable, depends essentially upon the legal context within which we are viewing it. Taken in the context of the more restricted local (or state) legal system, it is civil disobedience and it is not (in that system) legally justifiable. Taken in the context of the larger, federal legal system, the same act may be constitutionally justifiable, and if so it will not be viewed (in that system) as disobedient at all.

Uncertainty and confusion in the classification of particular protests is partly a consequence of a frequent and natural but unconscious shifting in thought from one to another of these contexts. Neither is *the* correct context; either may be appropriate depending upon the purpose of the judgment we seek to make. At times we view the act in the larger scheme of American law; at other times we view it in the smaller scheme of immediate law enforcement. In the former we may approve of the act, while in the latter we may conclude that, regrettably, it is a clear infraction of law and calls for legal action.

Once this shifting of context is recognized, a rational treatment of protests of this kind is greatly facilitated. Sound moral judgment of human conduct is rarely (if ever) possible without a thorough understanding of the context of fact and principle in which that conduct, and its judgment, goes on. As a practical matter, however, one should realize that the legal context of first and most pressing importance to one who deliberately breaks what he believes to be an unjust law is the immediate legal system within which that law is operative. While he may seek or believe himself entitled to ultimate constitutional justification, such a person is, in the immediate framework of law, guilty of some crime as a result of his deliberate act. In this primary context—very likely the only legal context in which his act will ever be formally judged—such a person surely is a direct civil disobedient. But in this context, of course, there is no legal justification for his act. Once again: no act can both violate the law and be justified by the law within the same legal system. (See also Chapters VII and VIII.)

CARL A. RUDISILL LIBRARY
LENOIR RHYNE COLLEGE

3. CIVIL DISOBEDIENCE AND MORAL JUSTIFICATION

It follows from what has been said that if there is any possible justification of civil disobedience it must come from outside the legal system. The disobedient protester, to justify his action, must give extra-legal reasons for breaking the law, and he must show that these nonlegal considerations override his obligation to obey the law. This will not be easy for him to do.

Let us put aside the case of a grossly immoral tyranny, of doubtful legitimacy, enforcing cruel and oppressive laws. Deliberate disobedience under such circumstances (if those circumstances could be agreed upon) might be generally and even readily approved. Such, however, is not the context in which most civil disobedients see themselves. They will allow, in most cases, that their government is a reasonably decent democracy, that it acts out of legitimate authority, and that its leaders are duly constituted. They will grant that the laws, having been properly authored and enacted by the people's representatives, have a legitimate claim on the obedience of all citizens, and that that claim applies to them, the disobedients, no less than to everyone else. This obligation to obey, however, is but one component of the moral forces acting upon them, they will argue. They are under other obligations also, strong moral obligations that outweigh those imposed by the legal system, and that constrain them to disobey certain laws under certain circumstances. While not claiming to be above the law, or exempt from it, they do claim to be *right* in disobeying it in very special and perhaps even agonizing situations.

Such claims are often mistaken and are sometimes out-rageous. They require careful defense. And the burden of the argument must rest upon the disobedient, since his deliberate violation of law must be presumed wrongful unless he can show why it is not. Further, his must be a rational defense. The mere allegation—even if it is in good faith—that one has a moral obligation to disobey cannot justify that disobedience. When the disobedient contends that in judging his act its circumstances as well as the letter of the law must be taken into account, he is correct. The moral obligations one is un-der and the resolution of conflicts among them do depend upon many complex considerations relating both to one's own circumstances and to his beliefs about those circum-stances, as well as to principles entirely independent of him. But while personal beliefs and circumstances are relevant, the final determination of what a man ought to do is dependent upon very much more than his own convictions, however sin-cere they may be. When the claim is made, therefore, that moral considerations compelled or justified disobedience of law, that claim needs to be closely examined in the light of the facts and principles that bear on the act in question.

Clearly there are at least some circumstances in which such a claim can be made good. We know that the laws, however much we labor to improve them, are never in full accord with our highest moral standards. Even under the best of legal systems law and morality may come into conflict. Sometimes the law may prove grossly unjust. Most systems, having sig-nificant imperfections, may occasionally encounter situations in which the conflict of law and justice is grave enough to justify a moral man's claim that he ought to break the law in protest. That "ought" cannot be a legal ought, of course. It is a moral claim for which, when pressed, the disobedient will be obliged to give weighty support. And whether or not he is able to make his case in the moral sphere, his act stands culpable and punishable before the law. We must admit, although never lightly, that there are some circumstances in which a man is morally justified in deliberately breaking the law.

Some cases of civil disobedience are of this sort; not all are. The exacting task is that of deciding which cases really are morally justifiable. Even if it does not affect the legal outcome, that determination is fundamental is passing judgment upon the character of the disobedient, and upon his conduct.

How might one go about justifying an act of civil disobedience? What forms might the reasoned defense of the morality of such conduct take? Specifically, they are many, nearly as many as the possible acts of civil disobedience themselves. Generally, however, there are two main paths the defender may follow. These two patterns of justification may prove mutually consistent in some cases, while in others the use of both may be impossible. Each civil disobedient, in any event, is likely to place ultimate reliance upon one or the other, depending upon his temperament and his philosophical convictions. It is very possible that a given disobedient may be confused on this subject. He may be mistaken about what grounds are best for the defense of his conduct, and he may even be uncertain about which pattern of justification would be his own ultimate recourse. He may not even clearly distinguish the two.

The two patterns are, nevertheless, very different, and they are in principle, if not always in practice, clearly distinguishable from one another. The first may be called *higher-law* justification; the second, *utilitarian* justification. I shall consider them in turn.

4. HIGHER-LAW JUSTIFICATION OF CIVIL DISOBEDIENCE

The civil disobedient may seek to justify his conduct by appealing to a law higher than any man-made law—a "divine" or "natural" law whose authority is supreme. Such laws, he may argue, impose duties so compelling that they override any conflicting obligations. Although the offending element of the positive law, the law of the state, be unambiguous and have general support, and even if it be the legitimate enactment of a legitimate government, if it commands an act forbidden by the supreme law of the universe it must be disobeyed. There is no right way to compromise with such supreme authority. It does not matter from what source the human opposition to it arises—King, or President, or Parliament. No act of human beings, whatever its form, can create an obligation strong enough to match the obligation imposed by the higher law.

This is a venerable line of argument, and it has often been employed by good men in the service of worthy causes. Its roots lie deep in the history of Western thought—in Cicero and Aquinas and Hooker and Grotius and Locke. It has become a prominent element in the American political tradition and underlies the epigram Jefferson hoped would be inscribed on the Great Seal of the United States: "Rebellion against tyrants is obedience to God." The civil disobedient

✎§ *Case 11. The recourse to higher-law justification for civil disobedience is also well illustrated by the case of James E. Wilson, whose story appeared in* The Catholic Worker *(March 1966). Having pleaded guilty to the charge of deliberately destroying his draft card, he was convicted and appeared in U.S. District Court in New York for sentencing on 4 March 1966. He made the following statement to the Court:*

On November 6, 1965, I did willfully and knowingly burn and destroy my draft-classification card, as my indictment by the Grand Jury reads. I did this only after great thought and prayer. It was performed as a religious act, and more specifically as a Christian act.

As a Christian I am opposed to all war and violence. I believe this is the teaching of Jesus Christ, and I must take this position if my conscience demands it. Although there are many who may disagree with my beliefs, I am sure they respect my right to hold them.

The duty and responsibility of every Christian is to stand up for Christ and speak out against injustice wherever it presents itself. We must do this even if it means breaking an existing law, for sometimes it is the law itself that is the injustice we must speak out against. The early Christians broke the law when they refused to swear allegiance to the Emperor in the Army of Rome. This was outright disobedience of an existing law which the

who employs this defense does not conceive his conduct to be rebellion, but very often the spirit of his act is precisely Jefferson's: when human law and divine law conflict, the moral man has no choice but to obey the latter, even if that entails deliberate disobedience of the former.

St. Thomas put the matter crisply: "Human law does not bind a man in conscience and if it conflicts with the higher law human law should not be obeyed." And the Second Vati-

Christians could not follow. There is a great tradition of disobedience to unjust laws in the history of Christianity. This is also true of the forefathers of this country, who were looking ahead to an ideal. When the Stamp Act was passed by England, the leaders of this land burned the stamps in direct defiance of the law.

I believe this law, under which I was indicted, is unjust. This is why I broke it, because it is unjust, and I cannot sit back and accept an injustice the way so many of us do, who then suddenly realize that every right has been slowly taken from us.

Is it necessary to prove that this law is unjust, or is it obvious to every Christian, or to anyone who looks to the Constitution of this country? I think it should be obvious to every one of us that this law cannot exist, and it cannot be given its existence by obedience. It cannot be ignored or honored. Rights have been taken from people on every corner of the earth because bad laws were shrugged off as not important, or because people thought the law did not affect them. This is why totalitarianism exists, and with the passing of this law we took a big step toward totalitarianism ourselves. If we remain silent now we must face the consequences tomorrow.

Does a man have a right to his own political or religious beliefs? Do we have a right to free and peaceful assembly? Is dissent a natural right of every human being? Do we have a right to free speech? These are the questions this law has raised. When we

can Council (1962), in harmony with contemporary Christians everywhere, was faithful to that tradition: "In the depths of his conscience man detects a law which he does not impose on himself but which holds him to obedience. . . . For man has in his heart a law written by God. To obey it is the very dignity of man." This conception of the supremacy of some divine or natural laws has had uncountable manifestations, formal and informal, in the political and religious documents, look to the Constitution we find that there is no doubt that this law is unjust. When we look to the Gospels we find out what we are to do when we are confronted with injustice. We *must* speak out! We *must* act!

This is what I have tried to do. This is why I broke the law, and for no other reason. I have pleaded guilty and will accept the consequences for what I have done. This protest which I have made does not end with the burning of an inexpensive piece of paper—it begins! The government have [sic] passed this law and now they must put it into practice. This is their responsibility, not mine. They must prove that this law exists while I prove it is unjust by my moral protest. This law must be enforced or it is in effect non-existent. I must force this issue on the government. They are big enough to make their own decision.

My freedom is very important to me. Freedom to walk through the streets of every city and catch the wind on my face. Freedom to gather with friends to drink ale and sing songs. Freedom to love people of every shape, color, and size. Freedom to bring joy to those who are sad, and sometimes the freedom to cry with those who are crying. These are the things that are important to me, and in order to keep them for myself and others, I will gladly go to jail. And others will follow me, and still others will follow them. For the free man and the Christian will soon realize that he will have to go to jail. So build more prisons and make them large, and we will all be together. The freedom that is tingling in my bones and in my soul cannot be held in by iron bars. ৵

speeches, and institutions of the West. Its history need not be reviewed.

Justification by resort to the higher law has been of fundamental importance to many (but not all) of those who, in recent years, have practiced civil disobedience in the United States. Martin Luther King, their most prominent spokesman, repeatedly presented this defense of such conduct. "One has a moral responsibility to disobey unjust laws," he said, and the difference between just and unjust laws is simply this:

A just law is a man-made code that squares with the moral law or the law of God. An unjust law is a code that is out of harmony with the moral law. To put it in the terms of Saint Thomas Aquinas: An unjust law is a human law that is not rooted in eternal and natural law. [Martin Luther King, Why We Can't Wait, Harper & Row, New York, 1963, pp. 84–85.]

King here goes on to argue, in defense of certain specific forms of civil disobedience, that any law that degrades human personality is unjust, that segregation statutes do just this, and that therefore they not only may but must be disobeyed. (See Case 11, pp. 106–108.)

Higher-law justifications bear some resemblance to the efforts, described earlier, to justify the disobedient act by showing that it is, when fully understood, in full harmony with the Constitution or otherwise protected by the ultimately controlling code. In those earlier cases, however, resort was made to laws or constitutional principles also man-made, but having greater authority than the law broken. So the appeal is made from the municipal to the state laws, or from the legal system of the state to that of the federated nation. All of these jurisdictions are alike, however, in having the authority only of human government; although one may overrule another, all are cut from what is basically the same cloth. Because the rulings of the higher courts specifically control the rulings of the lower courts, an act that is legally justified by the former cannot be forbidden or punished by the latter. All are parts of one greater legal system. Higher-law justification in the present sense is fundamentally different in that it appeals not merely to a superior element in the hierarchy but to another system entirely, whose origin and authority is entirely distinct from that of the system within which the law was broken. Because the laws of this higher system have (allegedly) a completely different and special character, not narrowly juridical, it is claimed that they can provide a purely moral justification of an act that is, in every sense, a clear and deliberate violation of the positive law.

Attempted moral justifications of this general kind may vary considerably in important detail; it is useful to distinguish the major forms such justifications take.

One great distinction is that between theological and non-theological higher laws. Advocates of the former—employing directly or indirectly the authority of God in their defense—are much the more common. Very many civil disobedients are quick to say that their act was in obedience to the law of God, while the law they broke was itself a violation of that law. Of course there may be difficulties in knowing what the law of God commands, or knowing how that command bears upon the case at hand. But while possibly recognizing the seriousness of such difficulties in some situations, these civil disobedients will deny that these problems arise in their own case. They will argue that the divine law is clearly written (in the Bible or some other holy book), or that it is expressed in all of Nature, or that it is indelibly imprinted within each man (on his heart, or mind, or soul), or that it is simply self-evident. In some form, depending upon the variety of religious conviction, the theological justification supposes that each civil disobedient knows the will of God and knows that He commands that disobedient act. The disobedient acknowledges this divine authority, obeys it, and is prepared to accept with fortitude whatever wordly punishment his act may receive.

The logic of higher-law justification, however, does not require a theological base. If the law appealed to is to have an authority greater than any human law or legal system, its source must indeed be superhuman. But it may be claimed that this superhuman source is not God or gods, but the Universe itself. The supreme moral law (according to this view) springs not from the will of persons, or some superior being, but is the inevitable product of the way things are. The supreme law is a "natural" law, but not a "divine" law. Its authority does not depend, therefore, upon the truth of any religious writings, or revelations, or beliefs. Its commands are universal and may be readily determined by each individual human being using (depending upon the variety of nontheological view) his reason, or his moral sense, or some other faculty, ordinary or special. This "natural" law is what the civil disobedient may invoke in seeking to justify his act.

The advocates of higher law, theological or nontheological, may quarrel bitterly about the true source of the moral commands (as historically they have done), and they may also be unable to agree upon the content of these commands. Or they may disagree in the former sphere, yet find themselves in general agreement in the latter. Or again; being in substantial if not complete agreement about what the supreme moral law commands, they may go on to claim that the distinction between theological and nontheological accounts is merely verbal—that talk about personal gods is only an allegorical way of talking about the Universe, or that the Universe is but another name for the one true God. In any case, what unites them at last is their conviction that there are universal moral laws, having a superhuman source and supreme authority, and that human beings know and understand these laws. Such laws may sometimes justify—morally, but not legally—the deliberate violation of a man-made statute.

A second distinction of interest, much less commonly drawn, is that between higher laws (whatever their origin) that are categorical and those that are criteriological. A law is categorical when it flatly commands or forbids certain categories of acts. "Never do so-and-so" or "Always seek to accomplish such-and-such results." This is the form higher laws are usually claimed to take when the object is justification of civil disobedience. To some, however, it appears easier and wiser to resort to higher authority not as a giver of categorical commands but as the source of criteria for moral judgment.

The justification is put in this softer way partly because of the abuse to which the stronger form is liable. If there is widespread resort to "higher law" as authority for disobedience, the proper powers of the civil authorities may be undermined. If it were generally believed that an individual through his personal understanding of the law of God (or Nature) might justifiably disobey the state, that would create, as the theologian Emil Brunner puts it, "an intolerable menace to the system of positive law." He continues: "No state can tolerate a competition of this kind presented by a second legal system. The laws of the state actually obtaining must possess a monopoly of binding legal force for itself [sic] if the legal security of the state is to remain unshaken." (Heinrich Emil Brunner, *Justice and the Social Order*, trans. by Mary Hottinger, Harper & Brothers, New York, 1945, p. 93.) But (according to this view) if we may not appeal to higher authority as a binding *law*, we may appeal to it as a *criterion*. Natural law does not command us to act in certain ways, but it remains nevertheless a moral standard for our conduct. We can, therefore, appeal to the standard of natural law in support of disobedience of positive laws we regard as so unjust that we cannot obey them in good conscience. In this way our conscience provides us with a criterion for conduct but is not itself law and does not exempt us from the governance of the law.

This distinction is of doubtful value. The aim in drawing it is to present the higher-law justification in a milder, less upsetting way. Lest it be thought that the recognition of the higher law will gravely weaken the necessary authority of normal government by establishing a competing juridical system, the higher authority is called "criterion" rather than "law." If natural law is not a legal system (it is suggested) it can pose no threat to the civil authorities. Whatever his conscience may require him to do, the moral man is still a citizen, and properly governed by the laws of his political community. But such talk about "criteria" instead of "laws" is a word screen only and does not really distinguish this approach from that which is more common and more direct. He who resorts to the moral law as a *law* recognizes at the same time that it is a law in a separate sphere, having separate foundations. Moral authority (according to this view) does not compete with civil government or in any way undermine it. It simply establishes certain very basic limits within which the civil government has the moral authority to operate. When the government exceeds these limits, the citizen is placed in a difficult position. He is then forced to act either illegally or immorally. If, in obedience to the higher law, he does break the positive law, he knows and all will agree that his act will be punished under the positive law. Nothing of real significance in this situation is changed by describing it as only a conflict between civil laws and conscience, or between legality and moral criteria of conduct. Whichever of these descriptions is chosen, the argument is essentially the same: there has been a resort to some superhuman authority to provide moral justification for an allegal act.

All of these justifications—theological and nontheological, criteriological and categorical—are efforts to resolve the dilemma facing a moral citizen who honestly believes that the civil law that governs him commands an immoral act. The resort to a higher authority, which all these arguments have in common, is very appealing. Such justifications of disobedience are simple, forceful, direct. Usually they manifest high personal integrity and require much courage. On the whole, however, these justificatory arguments, in spite of their emotional appeal, do not prove intellectually satisfactory.

The difficulties inherent in such arguments are many, but they reduce ultimately to two: (a) It appears impossible to reach any objective and reliable judgment about what the higher laws command or forbid (if there be any higher laws at all); and (b) It appears impossible to reach any objective and reliable judgment about how these laws (supposing their content known) apply to concrete cases, without resort to some established judicial authority. Just how these basic difficulties will enter in any given case will depend, of course, upon the variety of higher-law justification put forward.

The first of these obstacles the higher-law advocate often finds difficult to appreciate fully. Utterly convinced of the truth of his doctrine, and completely sure of its clarity and certainty, he is likely to think the refusal on the part of others to accept it is the result only of a deliberate and foolish blindness, or is perhaps partly disingenuous. He swears with all his heart to the truth of his Holy Writ and pities or wonders at the obtuseness of those who claim not to see the law of God written on the sacred page, or on the face of Nature, or in their own souls. Unfortunately, however deep and sincere their convictions, such advocates can provide nothing that will stand as publicly verifiable proof that the higher law is as they claim it to be. All of their evidence—of course they may claim tons of it—depends for its worth upon the reliability of their fundamental claims to knowledge of a special kind—through revelation, or moral intuition, or self-evidence, or some other. But it is just such special faculty or faculties that their skeptical critic is questioning in the first place. It is no reply to him to support the reliability of the alleged certainties with other claims having precisely the same foundation. If one questions whether a given book is the Word of God, it is not intellectually satisfying to be told that it must be the Word of God because it says so in that book. Or if one doubts the universality of a moral principle that another has claimed to intuit directly because he doubts the reality of that intuitive faculty, the questioner is most unlikely to be persuaded by the claim that he could intuit it himself if only he tried harder. In short, all partisans of the higher law face, at the outset, a grave epistemological barrier. They make knowledge claims that are practically impossible to defend. They pretend to know what the higher law demands of all men, but their argument, such as it is, is convincing only to those who already share their views. Many men—perhaps most men—do not share their views and cannot be given satisfactory rational grounds for acknowledging the authority of their alleged supernatural commands or criteria.

All higher-law arguments meet this problem, whatever their form or the alleged content of the law they invoke. Even if their principle is one receiving widespread approval and acceptance—say, "Thou shalt not kill"—the moment that principle is claimed to have a superhuman authority that justifies disobedience of law it is subject to the same fundamental doubt leveled at that claimed authority. Of course, the advocate of higher law may seek to bypass such doubts by resorting at last to some purely emotional appeal, or to some deliberately nonrational theology. He may indeed get converts in this way, but never a genuine justification of conduct.

The second obstacle met by higher-law justifications arises from the need to apply general laws or principles to specific situations, and from the uncertainties such applications necessarily engender. Supposing the statement of the higher law to be universally known and agreed upon (which is supposing a good deal), it yet remains to be determined how that law bears on the disobedient act in question. That is a matter notoriously difficult in any complex situation, and is, after all, one of the main reasons civilized communities establish and respect the authority of a judicial system in the first place.

The laws of the state are intended to be very clear—their framers strive for great accuracy and precision in formulation and often include detailed descriptions and definitions—and still their applications present the most trying problems for the courts. Judges learned and wise will often disagree upon practical applications of the same specific law or principle. The laws of God (or Nature), supposing them known, reach us in terms yet more general and less precise. "Thou shalt not kill," "Treat all men as equals," or other such principles, even if universally authoritative, are obviously subject to vastly different and conflicting interpretations. An individual relying upon such laws to justify his disobedience thereby claims for himself the power of interpretation and application that in the easier sphere of positive law is so carefully exercised and safeguarded by sophisticated legal institutions and carefully trained lawyers and judges. John Locke was among the greatest proponents of higher-law theories, yet even he insisted upon the fundamental need, in a civil society, for known (i.e., carefully written and promulgated) laws and known, impartial judges with independent power to enforce those laws. It is precisely the lack of these, he argued, that drives men (although governed by the natural law in some larger sense) to form civil governments, enact written legislation, establish courts of justice, and the rest. Now the civil disobedient, claiming the authority of the higher law as justification for his conduct, acts in a way that conflicts with the will and judgment of these civilized judicial institutions. He claims to be able to interpret the commands of that supreme authority with such sureness and rightness that no courts, or judges, or standard legal safeguards are needed by him. He knows the law; he knows how to apply it; that is the end of the matter. If he is pressed to show that his interpretation of the higher law is indeed correct, he can only fall back upon his own moral intuitions, or whatever other knowledge faculty he first claimed as the source of his moral inspiration. When he acts as judge in such matters, his analysis of conflicting laws and their applications in a specific case is likely to be debatable at the very least, if not grossly deficient and shallow.

All this if he is strictly impartial; in most cases he is subject to the additional distortions unavoidably introduced by the fact that it is his own case upon which he passes judgment.

No argument of this kind, moreover, can give satisfactory reply to the critic who, believing himself also governed by the divine code (or natural law, etc.), claims a sharply different and more accurate understanding of it. While agreeing that some variety of nonempirical knowledge is decisive, the two may flatly disagree about what their nonempirical sources say. No further court is open to them, since each will adamantly insist that the highest court of the universe has already decided the case for him. Whenever disobedient conduct—or indeed any political conduct—is defended on grounds such as these, the ensuing argument is likely to be irresoluble and bitter. In such conflicts the parties may soon be brought to that impasse at which they are forced to say: "Here ends the argument and begins the fight."

The resort to higher law is usually attended and encouraged by an understandable desire for certainty, universality, and justice. In practice, however, it necessarily becomes a resort to one's own convictions about God's will and how it must be carried out. What begins with a drive for universal objectivity ends, in this way, in a morass of idiosyncracy and subjectivity. Reliance upon supernatural codes, however described, gives shaky support for what are often sound principles that might prove entirely defensible on grounds that are wholly empirical but not absolute.

The obstacles facing any justification of civil disobedience by resort to higher law are indeed serious. It is very doubtful whether they can be overcome in a wholly rational way. The correctness of such a justification will be impossible to establish to the satisfaction of any who question its claimed epistemological foundations. By the same token, however, higher-law justifications cannot be wholly disproved either. Just as the ultimate evidence relied upon eludes public verification, so also it eludes public falsification. The defender of civil disobedience through higher law may stick to his claims in the face of all punishment and all objections. His critics *may* be suffering from some kind of moral blindness or corruption, and he *may* be right after all. But it will never be enough for him to claim that he may possibly be right. There is a burden of proof that lies upon him, the disobedient, and it is a very heavy burden to sustain.

Finally, the resort to higher laws in this context has a special shortcoming. These laws (as usually described) are of such a nature that they could serve to justify, if any, only *direct* civil disobedience—disobedience of the law that is itself the object of protest. The divine code, or law of nature, will address itself to specifically moral matters and not those that are mainly tactical. Whatever their particular content, therefore, the higher laws can justify disobedience only of statutes morally offensive in themselves. Much civil disobedience, however, is indirect, the law violated being not only distinct from the object of protest but in itself entirely wholesome and acceptable to the protester. The entire enterprise is then a political device in which the disobedience is used to speed a remedy for some more serious injustice in a related but separate sphere. The law to be broken will be selected openly by the demonstrators on prudential grounds, as one whose deliberate infraction might best advance their purposes. Such disobedience cannot be a direct consequence of divine command, nor can the indirect protest be reasonably defended as the unavoidable outcome of conflict between laws of nature and laws of men. If indirect civil disobedience is ever to be justified, something other than universal moral laws will have to be relied upon.

Some have been led to assert—perhaps partly because of their recognition of this limitation of higher-law justifications—that indirect disobedience never can be justified. But this claim begs the crucial question in that it tacitly supposes that justification by higher law is the only kind worthy of consideration. This is false, and it mistakenly forecloses the issue without opportunity for reflection upon other plausible and persuasive arguments the civil disobedient might present in his own defense.

5. UTILITARIAN JUSTIFICATION OF CIVIL DISOBEDIENCE

The second major pattern of justification is utilitarian. The term "utilitarian" is here used in a generous way, not necessarily tied to pleasures and pains, or to any specific calculus of goods and evils. It simply indicates that the justification will rely upon some intelligent weighing of the consequences of the disobedient act. The protester here argues, in effect, that his particular disobedience of a particular law, at a particular time, under given circumstances, with the normal punishment for that disobedience ensuing, is likely to lead in the long run to a better or more just society than would his compliance, under those circumstances, with the law in question. Making this claim is only the beginning; it needs to be thoroughly defended, and providing that defense will never be a simple matter. How successful such a defense may prove will depend not only upon the workability of its pragmatic form but upon the depth, and accuracy, and sophistication of the analysis of the consequences upon which it relies.

The protester who seeks to justify his deliberate disobedience along such lines necessarily faces a severe self-imposed handicap. Because he admits, as we have seen, that the law he breaks formally applies to him, his deliberate disobedience begins with a black mark against it. He must show that in spite of his acknowledged moral obligation to obey the laws, greatest long-range good is likely to result from disobedience in that given situation. Again, the burden is on him, and it is a heavy one.

In presenting this utilitarian justification of his conduct, the disobedient must employ two kinds of considerations, moral and factual. Here again it is unwise to construct a sharp dualism: moral principles accepted, or judgments made, are facts; and many facts have the highest moral import. But we can and should distinguish, in any given context, between the moral principles used in the evaluation of laws or conduct or social goals, on the one hand, and the factual calculations with which it is decided whether a certain law or line of conduct does accomplish or promote the goals sought. Roughly speaking, the distinction is that between ends and means. It is true that any act or institution may be viewed as either; but in any well-understood context there will be certain larger principles that function chiefly as evaluative, and a host of more detailed considerations whose importance is chiefly instrumental.

Because the civil disobedient seeks to justify his act morally, those larger evaluative principles are of fundamental importance to him. Fortunately for him, they are not likely to be the source of controversy between himself (the utilitarian civil disobedient) and his contemporary critics. It is almost invariably the case that he, like they, seeks a society in which all are treated equally by the laws and all are given equal opportunity for employment, housing, and the like. He, like they, abhors violence and opposes the aggressive use of military power. He hopes, as his critics do, to live in a community in which citizens are orderly, law-abiding, and free to live as they please within the law; he agrees with them in finding deliberate disobedience of law, taken by itself, intrinsically objectionable. The point requiring emphasis here is that the moral standards of these civil disobedients are normally as good as or better than those of their communities, and their moral principles are substantially shared by the vast majority of their fellow citizens.

The ultimate philosophical ground of these evaluative standards—whether religious, or metaphysical, or again pragmatic—while it may indeed prove a serious issue in other contexts, does not bear at all upon the disobedient's present argument. In this regard his procedure differs sharply from that of the higher-law advocate who bases everything upon the supremacy of the authority behind his laws. The utilitarian disobedient, in the context of providing a defense of his protest, has no need to resort to such authority (whether or not he would accept it), because the larger moral principles he employs *are* those of his community. Moral harmony in this sense is, happily, quite general these days.

In extraordinary cases, it is true, the civil disobedient may adopt moral standards in sharp conflict with those professed by his community. So a racist may engage in civil disobedience to protest racial integration, or members of some eccentric organization or party may practice civil disobedience to further their special ends. But such cases are rare, and when any coherent effort is made to defend them, it almost invariably turns out to be some form of higher-law defense. The utilitarian justification of disobedient protest the object of which is sharply out of harmony with the moral standards of the community as a whole is almost certain to fail. This is not to assume, of course, that the community is always right. But even if the community is wrong, and the eccentrics right, deliberate disobedient pursuit of their special objectives, as long as they are in a moral minority, is not likely to advance the protesters' goals, and hence not likely to be defensible on utilitarian grounds.

In any event, most disobedients—those who protest aggressive war, seek racial equality, or economic justice, or the like—when presenting a utilitarian defense of their protests, do so upon moral foundations that are both solid and very generally approved. This solidity and approval, indeed, is the key to their defense, when it is successful.

The controversy, therefore, arises not over what the civil disobedient is after but over how he goes after it. The disobedient (that he is a utilitarian disobedient will be for the present assumed) and his critics disagree about a host of factual matters connected with the protest. The critic is usually willing to allow, if he is honest, that the ideals of the protester are wholesome enough, even noble. But he won't allow that deliberately breaking the law in that way will advance those ideals, or will advance them enough to outweigh the wrongness of the disobedience itself. In principle it may be that the factual issues arising here could be resolved by an extensive and detailed analysis of the situation in which the protest takes place, including a deep historical examination of its background, and the most scientific estimate of its consequences, all pursued in the most impartial and scholarly spirit. In practice, however, the entering variables are so many, so complex, so difficult to measure, and so extended over time and place, as to render a clear resolution of the issues often impossible.

The success or failure of utilitarian justifications of civil disobedience, therefore, must always fall short of conclusiveness. In many cases the issue will remain very much in balance; in others the utilitarian case may pretty clearly fail; in still others it may pretty clearly succeed. The very nature of the utilitarian argument, requiring the rational balancing of many conflicting considerations, serves as warning that a definitive result will most often be an unreasonable expectation.

Without a thorough understanding of the actual context of an act of civil disobedience it is impossible to identify, much less weigh, the factual considerations central to the utilitarian defense of that act. Philosophical analysis, if not restricted in applicability to a particular case of disobedience, or a specific context, must pay for its generality by remaining less than decisive in many concrete instances. The philosophical character of utilitarian justifications of civil disobedience can be probed more deeply, however, by identifying the major spheres within which complex issues of fact are likely to arise, and by specifying the kinds of questions likely to be raised within each sphere.

The first set of issues concern the *background* of the case at hand. How serious is the injustice whose remedy is the aim of the disobedient protest? How pressing is the need for that remedy? How vigorously and how intelligently has that remedy been sought through normal channels—party caucuses, legislative lobbying, and the like? Have extraordinary but lawful means—assemblies of protest, letter-writing campaigns, etc.—been given full trial? If all channels within the law have not been explored, or have not been explored fully enough, the resort to law-breaking is almost sure to prove unjustifiable. Finally, though the answer be always uncertain, we must ask what reasonable expectation there might have been, given previous efforts, that some remedy could yet be achieved through the continued use of lawful channels already tried.

A second set of factual questions concern the *negative effects* of the deliberate disobedience. Here we should distinguish between short-range and long-range consequences, of which the former are easier (but not easy) to assess. How serious will be the inconvenience caused other citizens who are not to blame for the wrong protested? How great is the expense incurred by the community as a consequence of the disobedience? Some such inconvenience and expense is unavoidable, but its degree may vary enormously. Is any violence entailed or threatened by the disobedient act? And if so, to property or to persons? If there is a threat to persons, justification of the act may be practically out of the question, and some may refuse even to classify it as civil disobedience. (See Chapter I, Section 8.) Even if not violent, what is the likelihood that some injury to persons or property may ensue as an *indirect* result of the protest? Increase in the probability of such injury will render the disobedience that much harder to justify. Long-range negative consequences would comprise all injuries—most of them intangible—to the order or spirit of the community. Has a bad example been set, a spirit of defiance or hooliganism encouraged? Has respect for law been decreased in the community, or the fundamental order of the society disturbed? Has democracy been subverted, or the political processes of democracy in that community damaged? These questions are complex and difficult to answer, yet they are of central importance in determining how much evil the disobedient act incurs, and hence are also central to its utilitarian justification. (See Chapter VI.)

The third and final set of questions concern the *positive effects* of the disobedient protest. It is undertaken, after all, with good and not evil intentions; fairness requires that in appraising it we weigh the good as well as the evil consequences. Both short- and long-range factors enter here too, but the former are few in number. If the disobedience is direct, and the law broken really is immoral, some immediate good will be done through the refusal to commit the wrongful act; we must ask how valuable that refusal is, in itself and as an example to others who may be encouraged by it to resist evil themselves. Whether direct or indirect, the disobedience is almost certain to result in some immediate public attention—first to the protester and then to the object of his protest. In a democracy, public attention to controversial matters of public concern is a good thing; but we must ask how valuable this resulting publicity is. Again, long-range positive results will be extremely difficult to assess. Suppose that the change the disobedient has in view is a genuinely worthy one. How much influence will his protest have in accomplishing that change? Can that civil disobedience bring significant pressure to bear upon law-making or policy-making authorities having the power to enact the change? If such pressure cannot be brought to bear directly, can it be done indirectly, by focusing public attention upon a community injustice long in need of remedy? How effectively can disobedient protest attract public attention to the object of protest? If it is so attracted, what is likely to be the outcome? Will the public, in turn, exert pressure upon the law-makers? Or will misunderstanding of the demonstrators, and resentment of them, cause more harm than good? One reason for the great difficulty of these questions is that their answers require a rational estimate of the future reactions of a large body of citizens to a chain of complex and controversial events. No one can know what those reactions will be, and every such estimate—even when in retrospect—may be very wide of the mark.

This third set of questions makes it clear, too, that the justification of the disobedient protest is much affected by the effectiveness of that protest. And its effectiveness, in turn, is much affected by a number of other factual aspects of the situation, some of which are these:

(a) The nature of the law broken. First, how grave is the crime actually committed? It is one thing to commit a deliberate trespass, quite another to interfere with the movement of a troop train, or to refuse to pay one's taxes. And second, if the disobedience is indirect, is the law broken so related to the object of protest as to make the point and seriousness of the demonstration abundantly clear to the general public? If it is not, its effectiveness drops sharply.

(b) The demeanor of the demonstrators. Unruly or offensive behavior is likely to be condemned out of hand; its larger objectives may then be obscured from public attention, or conveniently ignored by the press, which is likely to focus on the most sensational aspects of the demonstration. Conduct that is sober and restrained is more likely to win consideration and respect, to force the reflection of the public, and thereby to increase the effectiveness of the disobedient protest.

(c) The precise nature of the goal. How effective a protest is judged to be depends very largely upon what it is expected to accomplish. If its objective is limited—say, that of calling dramatic attention to a community wrong, with an expressed trust in the power of the public will when that wrong is recognized and understood—a considerable measure of success might be hoped for. If the protest is judged only in terms of its immediate success in pushing through the desired change in law or policy—racial desegregation, or the immediate cessation of hostilities in some war, etc.—it is likely to be deemed a failure. Not simply "How effective is it?" but rather "How effective is it for what end?" is the question to be asked.

All of these and more are the issues likely to arise when the effort is made to justify, in some utilitarian way, any single instance of civil disobedience. It is obvious that even the attempt at such a justification must be a very complicated affair.

✌ VI ⧫

SEVEN ARGUMENTS AGAINST
CIVIL DISOBEDIENCE

1. THE VARIETIES OF ATTACK

Two patterns possibly usable for the justification of civil disobedience have been roughly sketched out. Their actual use, of course, will be by particular individuals in particular contexts, defending particular acts of civil disobedience. But can that defense ever be successful? Many hold that it cannot. It is time to examine the arguments put forward by those who maintain that civil disobedience is never justifiable.

The aim of what follows should be very clear from the start. It is certainly not to defend all cases of civil disobedience; obviously not all cases are defensible. Rather it is my object to show that many arguments, very commonly met, which seek to demonstrate that civil disobedience cannot ever be justified, do not accomplish that. Some of these arguments will succeed against some cases of civil disobedience; none will succeed in every case.

The order imposed on these arguments must be somewhat artificial. In common political discourse they are often mixed together, confused one with another. I shall try to clarify them, and to do so by presenting them as persuasively as I can, for I believe they embody much sound criticism. But it is also my intention to identify their weaknesses and to show that these arguments are neither so powerful nor so sweeping in effect as their proponents commonly believe.

One variety of argument, of philosophical importance, I will mention at the outset but not discuss except incidentally. These are the arguments directed against one or the other of the general schemes of justification earlier laid out. Many critiques have aimed to show the unavoidable weaknesses in the epistemological foundations of any higher law (or "natural law") system. I have discussed these briefly (see Chapter V, Section 4) and will not return to them. Other philosophical critiques, equally numerous, have aimed to show the necessary failure of every essentially utilitarian or pragmatic approach to moral questions. I do not make light of these very general arguments, but there are good practical reasons to bypass them here. Most of the critics of civil disobedience, although they may not have expressed definitive positions on these underlying epistemological questions, will be in general sympathy with one or the other of the major alternative approaches. It will not be the utilitarian approach that some decry but rather its application in defense of deliberate law-breaking. For others it will not be the general reliance upon higher laws that they decry but the claim that such laws can justify knowing disobedience of the civil authorities. So it is not the very general arguments against utilitarianism or natural law but the more restricted arguments against civil disobedience itself that are the proper objects of concern here.

Some of these arguments are framed with the higher-law defender, and some with the utilitarian defender, chiefly in mind; most do not make that distinction clearly if at all. Some of these arguments are aimed at direct disobedience and some at indirect disobedience; most do not draw this distinction either. Some of these arguments are superficial and poor; some are entirely reasonable but of very limited applicability; a few are subtle and require the most careful consideration. I shall formulate them as fairly as I can.

2. FIRST ARGUMENT:

Civil Disobedience Implies Contempt for the Law

Persons who engage in civil disobedience deliberately flout the law; they make light of it in a way that cannot be justified in a law-governed community.

This is among the most frequently heard criticisms of civil disobedients, and it is among the weakest. Although the manner of civil disobedients is sometimes defiant, their conduct is more often a manifestation of respect for law than of contempt for it. Realizing that the law he breaks applies to him, the civil disobedient violates it knowingly in an effort to correct what he believes to be a wrong infinitely worse than the one he commits, and thereby to improve the system of laws. He understands that such deliberate violation of law will be met with legal punishment, and he does not normally seek to evade that outcome. It cannot be too strongly emphasized that civil disobedience is usually a tactic aimed at effecting needed changes through deliberate and public self-sacrifice. The disobedient breaks the law *and is punished*. He may

❧ *Case 12. This spirit of deliberate and honest self-sacrifice is well illustrated by the following actual cases.*

(a) An American Quaker and devoted pacifist, Fred Moore, Jr., applied to his draft board for classification as a conscientious objector. He received this classification in April 1964. Later he told Bill Davidson of the Saturday Evening Post ("Hell, No, We Won't Go," January 1968) that at the time of its receipt he had "a strange reaction to the notice. I had no feeling of relief or gladness. Instead, I had the feeling that I was a moral coward, and that I had ended up cooperating with the Selective Service system in order to get special status for myself." He sent his 1-O classification card back to his draft board, advising them that they were participating in "the march toward totalitarianism." He began lecturing on peace at college campuses over the country and wore sandwich boards reading: "Liberty, Yes; Conscription, No," "Thou Shalt Not Kill," and "Don't Dodge the Draft; Oppose It."

Having refused all cooperation with the Selective Service system, he was ordered to surrender himself at the United States Court-

expect that the punishment meted out to him will be (rightly or not) more severe than that inflicted upon less principled offenders of the same law. His suffering this punishment, his humiliation and probable maltreatment, are essential parts of his protest. It is not simply the breaking of the law as such but the entire demonstration, the preparation for it and its aftermath, that serves as his public declaration of anguish over a continuing community injustice. (See Case 12.)

In accepting punishment the civil disobedient further demonstrates his respect for the system of laws—a system he seeks to better and strengthen, not subvert or destroy. Most civil disobedients have been very clear about this, making no issue of their technical guilt of the crime with which they are charged. (See Chapter IV, Section 3.) But the practice here *house in Alexandria, Virginia, which he did, going on trial for draft evasion on 21 October 1965. Refusing court-appointed counsel and defending himself, he told the Court that he could not plead guilty because the draft was on trial and not he. He argued that conscription was a form of involuntary servitude, prohibited by the 13th Amendment, and was therefore unconstitutional. He was found guilty and sentenced to two years in federal penitentiary. He waived his right to appeal.*

Two days after completing his sentence at the Allenwood Federal Prison Camp, he was active on an antiwar picket line. He joined a group called Quaker Action, helping to send medical supplies to both North and South Vietnam. When he received a new draft classification card, showing conscientious objector status, he burned it, expecting to be prosecuted a second and perhaps a third time. He said: "I'm perfectly willing to go to jail again for my beliefs."

(b) Richard Boardman, a pacifist from Chicago, originally held a draft deferment on the basis of conscientious objection. After

does vary, depending chiefly upon whether the disobedience is direct or indirect. If direct, the protester may argue that the law he broke was itself immoral, and he may therefore press his case in the courts, seeking ultimate constitutional support and the quashing of the offensive statute. (See Chapter V, Section 2.) If his disobedience was indirect, the law he broke may itself meet his full approval, and he is likely to admit his legal guilt. In the latter case especially he may view his punishment as the tactical culmination of his protest. In neither case does his conduct justify the criticism that it shows "contempt" for law, or "makes light" of the law. That criticism badly misapprehends the nature of the disobedient's acts and disregards his publicly stated intentions. (See Case 13.)

long and anguished reflection he decided that he could no longer retain that status in good conscience and wrote his local Selective Service Board a long, thoughtful, and respectful letter explaining why he would no longer comply with any directives from the Selective Service system. (See "Letter to Local Board No. 114," Richard M. Boardman, reprinted in Civil Disobedience: Theory and Practice, ed. by Hugo Adam Bedau, Pegasus Books, New York, 1969, pp. 178–86.) In this letter he explains that he understands that in following this course of action he is breaking the law, and that he deeply regrets that. Compliance with the law, however, makes him an agent of injustice (he argues) and forces upon him an hypocrisy he cannot tolerate. He urges the Board to seek to understand the agonies of one in his moral position. Later in 1967 he told a reporter (see magazine article referred to in 12 (a), above): "This is my country, and I love it, and I will stay here and go to jail if necessary to help correct its mistakes. I accept the general framework of the law, and I accept the penalties for breaking the law." ⧼⧽

3. SECOND ARGUMENT:
Civil Disobedience Supposes the Primacy of Selfish Interests

No act of civil disobedience can be morally justified, because every such act is immoral at base, in supposing the superiority of individual to social interests. The civil disobedient acts out of self-regard, in deliberate defiance of the will of his community, and that can never be right.

This criticism, like the one before it, is superficial and unfair; it assumes the act of disobedience to have a character it does not have. Like the preceding argument, it tacitly supposes that the civil disobedient does not care what the law requires—when in fact he cares very much. It tacitly suggests that the civil disobedient hopes to be able to defy the law ᴥ§ *Case 13. The spirit of deep respect for the laws and for justice, as manifested by many civil disobedients, is beautifully illustrated by one classical conflict between Jewish law and Roman authority. The ancient historian Josephus, in his The Wars of the Jews (Book Two, Chapter 10) relates the following events.*

Caius Caesar thought himself a god, and insisted upon being treated as one. To this end he had statues of himself placed, for worship, in the temples of conquered nations. Continuing in this practice, he sent Petronius, with three Roman Legions and many Syrian auxiliaries, from Antioch to Judaea to set up his statues in the temples of the Jews. His orders were to put to death any who interfered with the emplacement of the icons. As the news spread panic spread also. Josephus then continues with this account (from The Works of Flavius Josephus, translated by Dr. Hudson, published by Janeway's, London, 1732):

The Jews, with their wives and children, presently assembling together in the plain, warmly sollicited Petronius, first, for the laws of their country, and then for themselves; but he not any ways molified with the earnest sollicitations of the people, left his

without punishment, if he can get away with it—which is also usually false.

This argument has the additional fault, however, of supposing that the civil disobedient does what he does to advance his private interests, pursuing those interests with a callous disregard for the legal rights of others. In most cases nothing could be further from the truth. Normally the civil disobedient does not further his selfish interests at all; indeed, most often he knowingly does damage to his private interests and perhaps those of his family. Sometimes that damage is serious. He is certain to be greatly inconvenienced, to have his home life as well as his work or studies disrupted repeatedly.

army and the statues in Ptolomais; and then going into Galilee, and assembling the people, and some of the principal natives at Tiberias, he laid open to them, in a long speech, the great power of the Romans, and the menaces of Caesar, and shewed them how vain and ridiculous their petition was. For after all the nations that were subject to the Roman empire had set up in their several cities the statues of Caesar among their other Gods, that the Jews should be the only persons to refuse it, argued a great sign of disaffection, and was an action full of the most open contumely.

When they had alledged in their defence their ancient constitution, the laws and customs of their country, and had urged the unlawfulness of setting up in the temple any image representing God or man, or putting them up in any other prophane place of their country; Petronius immediately answered, "But I," said he, "must necessarily obey the decree of my master, and if I act contrary to it, and spare you, my life will certainly be made the price of my disobedience. He himself who hath sent me, and not I, will then besiege you; for I, as well as you, am subject to his authority." The whole multitude hereupon cried out, that they would suffer the worst torments to preserve their laws. Petronius

Very probably he will be publicly condemned and embarrassed. He runs some risk of physical abuse, both from arresting police officers who may not be gentle and from provoked onlookers who may not be rational. Worst of all, he incurs the permanent burden of a criminal record, a serious handicap especially for a young member of the middle class. Throughout his life he may be obliged to explain the circumstances of his arrest; and his conviction may cost him dearly in employment opportunities lost and in loss of the right to practice some professions. These penalties are accepted by the disobedient not gladly but willingly, as probable consequences of an effective protest. The complaint that the civil having appeased their clamour, said, "Are you in a condition to maintain a battle against Caesar?" To which the Jews replied, "Twice a day we offer sacrifice for Caesar, and the Roman people; but if his intentions are arbitrarily to set up the statues, his first business should be to make a general sacrifice of the whole nation of the Jews, for, as for our selves, we were ready with our wives and children to offer our throats to any that will cut them." From this moment Petronius began to admire and pity them, who were so resolute in defence of their religion, and so steadily prepared to yield to death. In short, for this time they were dismissed without any resolution being taken against them.

Josephus goes on to relate that Petronius continued to argue with those who so defied the Roman law. He exhorted them, threatened them, pleaded with them that he had no choice in the matter. But the Jews were adamant, and in the end he gave in, out of admiration for them, and returned with his army to Antioch. Hearing what he had done, Caius Caesar replied in anger, repeating his order and threatening Petronius with death. But that response was nullifed by the timely death of Caesar himself. ꝫ

disobedient acts chiefly out of self-regard is either disingenuous or flows from great ignorance.

The case of direct disobedience by those who deliberately break laws seriously restricting their own freedom is admittedly somewhat more complicated. In these cases some immediate personal benefit does accrue to the disobedient as a result of his act, and that fact is likely to cast some doubt upon the sincerity of his moral complaints and will encourage the criticism that the disobedience was selfishly motivated. The fact of that immediate benefit does not prove selfishness, however. A more careful weighing of all the probable consequences of the act (which the disobedient is very likely to have made) will show that even in such cases the disobedient protester knowingly opens himself to penalties and indignities far greater than those he would suffer if he remained obedient to the law he believes immoral. The best illustration here is the case of one who, believing military conscription laws immoral, refuses to cooperate with such laws in any way, and refuses induction. He will escape military service, but at fearful cost. In addition to arrest, humiliation, expense, and criminal record, he may spend at least two years, possibly five years, and probably three or more years in a federal penitentiary. (See Case 14.)

It is possible that a few persons may sometimes deliberately disobey certain laws, with their own advantage in mind, in the guise of practicing civil disobedience. That is a most imprudent course from their own standpoint and will be quickly abandoned by those selfishly inspired. When all the consequences have been reckoned the civil disobedient cannot reasonably be said to have advanced his private interests. The argument that his protest cannot be justified because he places these interests above the welfare of his community is doomed to fail in most cases.

4. THIRD ARGUMENT:
Civil Disobedients Take the Law into Their Own Hands

Every attempt to justify civil disobedience must fail, because all such efforts depend, at some point, upon a fundamental premise that is false—the premise that every man is entitled to decide for himself which laws he is to obey. A good society is necessarily governed by laws having known and general application. In supposing that the civil disobedient may assume the right to ignore these laws, to take the law into his own hands, his defenders must

✑ *Case 14. The prison sentence imposed for conviction of the felony "failure to report for induction" may range from a minimum of six months to a statutory maximum of five years. Fines may be imposed additionally, but rarely are. In practice, the prison sentences received by civil disobedients convicted of Selective Service violations are usually longer than their term of military service would have been. In many cases they are much longer. One severe instance is that of Clifton Haywood, a civil disobedient in Georgia who twice refused to report for induction on grounds of conscience. In passing sentence upon him, the Federal judge said: "I am going to adjudicate him guilty and there are two offenses I can find him guilty on. I am going to give him five years on the first and five on the second, making a total of 10,000 dollars and ten years. We can't fool around with people like that. We are in a war and a man who is a citizen of this country ought to act as such. (Haywood v. U.S., 393 F2d 780, 1968.) The case was twice appealed on procedural grounds. This degree of harshness is exceptional, but the possibility of lengthy prison sentence is very real for every disobedient of this kind.* ✑

employ a principle that is not only false but pernicious. Even allowing that his motivation may be honorable and not self-seeking, and even granting that his manner is not willful and defiant but sober and restrained, the citizen has not got the moral right to choose for himself whether to obey or not to obey the laws of his community.

Although this common argument seems clear, and carries some initial plausibility, it is in fact rather confused and not nearly as persuasive upon examination as it appears superficially. Essentially the argument is a denial of the claim that the citizen has, under any circumstances, the right to choose to disobey the laws of his community. That sounds simpler than it is. If one asks for a more precise identification of what is being denied, he will see that this critical argument is ambiguous, that it is open to two quite different interpretations —and that according to neither of these interpretations does the argument have the general force it claims.

The first interpretation of the argument places the emphasis on the mental act of the agent, his choice. A citizen hasn't the right to *choose* to obey or disobey the laws. To permit such choice (those who hold to this view suppose) is to give so much power to individuals that all state or community authority is undermined.

But this is false. Whatever may be the particular laws having rightful authority in a community, the persons over whom that authority is exercised, if they are free men, not only may choose but *must* choose, at many important junctures in their lives, between obedience to and disobedience of these laws. That a given statute is a law of their community, duly enacted by some constituted authority, is indeed one great factor in determining their moral duty; when the community is just, and the authority legitimate, good citizens will almost invariably decide that obedience is their moral obligation. Obedience to such legitimate authority conveniently and properly becomes a matter of habit in a well-ordered community.

Good habits developed in one set of circumstances may result in wrong acts, however, when followed unreflectively even after the circumstances have been drastically altered. Although obeying the law is generally a very good thing, and we do well to encourage its habitual practice, the mere fact that some act is commanded by a law is not in every case an absolutely controlling moral consideration. Moral citizens must sometimes decide for themselves whether other ethical factors override that consideration, and hence must decide whether they will obey particular laws. Even when their deliberations result in obedience, that obedience may often (and rightly) be a *decision* made by them. Indeed, obedience, though habitual as a practical necessity in many cases, is most moral and most honorable when undertaken as the deliberate consequence of rational reflection upon one's several (possibly conflicting) obligations. The case of disobedience is not different in this respect. It may be malicious or well-intentioned; it may prove objectively wrong or right; but the disobedient act—just like the obedient one—is often the outcome of a deliberate and thoughtful decision, a *choice* made by the actor.

To argue, therefore, that citizens do not have the right to choose in this sphere is a bad mistake; it involves a misconception of the character of the moral life entirely, giving to state authority a role in human life far greater than it deserves. If men may never choose between obedience and disobedience they become wholly subject to the whim of the state or other law-making authorities. Deliberation and intelligent self-guidance are then virtually excluded in any matters upon which some law has been enacted. Not only does this sharply reduce the sphere of genuinely moral conduct but it drains the public sphere of the morality it desperately needs. If every law must be obeyed in every situation, without exception, the practice of obedience itself must lose its reflective character, and the role of thoughtful citizen is replaced by the role of thoughtless slave. In decent communities this does not happen. Citizens are not slaves, and the proof of it is that they *choose* to act as they do—obeying the laws with pride in the vast majority of cases, and in some situations disobeying deliberately out of moral conviction.

Ambiguity in the phrasing of this argument is partly responsible for obscuring both its own weakness and the real moral quality of the civil disobedient's act. "No citizen may choose to disobey the law" the critic says, and he is right if he means to condemn the exercise of a moral option guided by nothing more than the agent's whim or pleasure. In that capricious sense, of course, the citizen has no right to choose to disobey. But deliberative choice is another matter entirely, and that is the kind of choice the civil disobedient makes. If this argument boils down to the denial to moral citizens of the right of such deliberative choice, it is a very bad argument indeed.

The second interpretation of this argument places emphasis on the issue of applicability of the law. The disobedient thinks himself entitled (the argument is now understood to state) to decide for himself whether a given law applies to him, whether he is under its jurisdiction. This determination (the critic continues) he cannot be authorized to make, because laws are necessarily general in their application, deriving their legitimacy from a communal act, not from the agreement of each individual singly.

This point is well made. But if in fact it be the nub of the argument in hand, it simply does not apply to most civil disobedients. They recognize clearly and admit publicly that, in both ordinary and technical senses, the law they break does apply to them. It is in the face of this application (and sometimes because of it) that they hold themselves justified in disobeying a given law—either in view of its irreconcilability with some higher principle or in view of the long-range good their disobedience is believed likely to produce. Here again, the critic of civil disobedients misses his target by supposing them to ignore what in fact they weigh (however accurately) with great care. Particular justifications of civil disobedience, of course, may not stand up. The disobedient may be much mistaken about the higher principle he invokes, or may grossly overestimate the good he will accomplish. But in either case his act is a deliberative one, and his deliberations *include* the force of his obligations to obey the laws in general and this law in particular. It is therefore simply a mistake to argue that the civil disobedient decides what laws apply to him. That is a community decision, and he recognizes it as such. His decision, sometimes the result of agonizing deliberation, concerns which laws, if any, among all those applying to him, he must disobey. That is a decision every citizen must be prepared to make if he is not to default in his role as a moral man.

To be fair to this argument, however, there is one special category of civil disobedience (or quasi-civil disobedience) that is sometimes defended on the ground that the law broken does not apply to the person who (apparently) breaks it. Whether the argument holds against this variety of disobedience I am not sure. This disobedience arises in the following way. Many thoughtful people maintain that one is genuinely obligated to obey only those laws in whose making one had a real voice, or the genuine opportunity to express one's voice. Democracy alone is truly legitimate government (according to this view); all other authority is unjustly imposed and cannot require—in any moral sense—the obedience of the citizen. Now it happens that in some political communities democracy, although professed, is grossly imperfect in that large minorities—usually racial or ethnic—are permitted little or no effective voice in framing the laws purporting to govern them. In some cases members of a highly visible minority may be wholly and deliberately excluded from the law-making process. When that happens—as it often has, and sometimes does still in the United States—a member of that excluded minority may argue on purely democratic grounds that he has no obligation to obey the laws so enacted. Having had no opportunity to participate in making them, he claims no duty to respect them; if he is to be treated as outside the community when the laws are framed, then, in justice, he should be outside it also when the laws are enforced. Such laws do not, he argues, apply to him at all, and his disregard of their commands is not disobedience in his own eyes, whatever it may be for others.

Whether this is a satisfactory defense of the deliberate disregard for laws is a question whose answer requires—what cannot be given here—a fuller analysis both of democracy itself and of the facts of the case of alleged exclusion from the democratic process. Two points about this defense of (apparent) disobedience should be made, however. The first is that, even in these special cases, the decisions of such a person to act without regard for the laws of a community from which he has been excluded is necessarily a reflective one. Whether the laws do apply to him is not, by his own argument, simply a matter of his think-so but a question of objective principles and facts. His principles may be in error; but he will seek to defend them rationally and then to apply them honestly to the facts he believes demonstrable. Even if badly mistaken at some point in his analysis, he cannot be justly accused of lightly choosing to disobey or to opt out of the society. Second, and more important here, one should note that such cases are really marginal for present purposes, because they are not true instances of civil disobedience at all. These acts are not performed within a frame of legal authority recognized by the actor; these persons specifically deny that they are within the jurisdiction of the law disregarded, and they will therefore consistently evade or combat arrest or punishment, which they regard as illegitimate for persons in their circumstances. Civil disobedience is self-consciously *disobedient*; in these special cases the acts are not (in the view of the actors) disobedient at all.

To say that such cases are not truly civil disobedience does not minimize their importance, deny their reality, or hide their growing number. Many are the members of American minorities—Negroes and Indians for two—who increasingly come to believe that the laws of the political community have little if any claim upon *their* obedience, in view of their treatment in the making of these laws. As such feelings become more widespread and intense, the community is faced with inevitably increasing disorder. Not civil disobedience but rebellion against (alleged) unjust authority is the proper description of such conduct. That the authority—and hence the demand for obedience—is indeed unjust is clear in some cases, unclear in many others. The issues go far beyond civil disobedience.

5. FOURTH ARGUMENT:
Civil Disobedience Undermines Respect for the Law

Now we must face an argument that has considerable persuasive power. Essentially it is the contention that civil disobedience is so fundamentally damaging to the welfare of

the society that no justification of it can succeed. It is necessary to distinguish two major variants of this attack, the first
directed against defenses of civil disobedience that rely ultimately upon some higher law and the second against those
that rely upon some utilitarian calculus. I call these variants
the "social-chaos argument" and the "social-fabric argument,"
respectively, and shall discuss them in turn.

The Social-Chaos Argument. In this version the attack is
directed not only against civil disobedience itself but also
against the higher-law systems sometimes used to defend it.

*Civil disobedience that is defended by seeking to invoke some
higher (or "natural") law beyond and above the systems of positive
law and alleged to have universal and supreme authority always
proves unjustifiable at last. This is because the very nature of this
defense is a serious threat to a stable social order. An effective
system of laws, and the peaceful and orderly life of a community
under the laws, is possible only when the authority of those laws
is not readily overthrown by appeal to some principles outside the
legal system. Where the right to such appeal is vested in each
citizen, and the only criteria for the judgment of this appeal are
his understanding of the alleged higher principle and his interpretation of its application to the case at hand (which is likely
to be his own case), legal authority is readily overthrown, and
social chaos, although not inevitable, is threatened and to some
degree invited. So grave is this consequence that civil disobedience
that relies upon the universal availability of such appeals can
never be justified.*

There are several things wrong with this argument. In the
first place, historical evidence does not support the claim that
appeal to some higher law leads to chaos. It is true that social
disorder has sometimes followed the appeal to such laws, but

it cannot be inferred that the appeals were the causes of disorder; more likely, both the appeal and the disorder were the product of social conditions that had become intolerable. On the whole, the Western—and particularly the American—political tradition is greatly indebted to philosophers who advocated such appeals under some circumstances, and to courageous leaders who relied upon such appeals to justify their battles for a better society. In theory and in practice, the appeal to a higher law, although sometimes badly abused, has most often been the instrument of persons or movements with noble and socially desirable objectives. Its actual use has most often brought not chaos but an improved political order.

In the second place, it is not even true that the reliance upon a higher law has any natural tendency to result in social chaos. This is because higher laws are almost invariably believed to require obedience to the legally constituted authorities except under the most extraordinary circumstances. Only when the offense of those authorities against that higher law is perfectly clear, perfectly wrongful, and morally intolerable, is such law likely to be invoked in defense of deliberate disobedience of the positive law.

In the third place, the fact that the appeal to a higher law may be misused, through error or by design, and thereby disrupt the social order on some occasions, does not prove such an appeal always inappropriate or insufficient. However unsympathetic one may be to higher-law justifications, and however distrustful of individual judgments regarding the content, authority, and applicability of such laws, fairness compels the admission that their mistaken use (or even deliberate misuse) cannot show that higher laws do not bind a man, or all men, to disobey some positive laws under some circumstances. Justifications through appeals to higher law may in fact be weak and generally unreliable (see Chapter V, Section 4), but from that we may not conclude either that they are always out of order or that social chaos is their natural consequence.

In the fourth place, even were the premise of the argument granted (that resort to higher laws does destroy, or tend to destroy, an effective system of positive laws), the conclusion (that civil disobedience so defended can never be justified) does not follow. It is not difficult to imagine (or remember) cases in which the injustice of the positive laws is so intolerable, the acts they command so atrocious, that one has, even in the face of the disorder one's appeal may encourage, an absolute duty to disobey.

I conclude that, on one or more of these grounds, the social-chaos variant of the fourth argument fails. It is properly voiced as a warning to those who, in pursuit of good but relatively minor objectives, do not fully appreciate the importance of a stable legal order—but it cannot establish that obedience to that order is a duty in every case supreme.

The Social-Fabric Argument. In this variant the attack is not against the utilitarian pattern of defense but, within that pattern, against the damaging nature of civil disobedience itself.

Civil disobedience defended in some utilitarian or pragmatic way can never be justified in the end, for the most careful weighing of its good and bad results must invariably show the long-range balance to be negative. This is not because of the inconvenience and expense to the community that the disobedient knowingly causes as an unavoidable byproduct of his act. Sometimes these are so great as to show the disobedience unjustifiable on its face;

but admittedly cases of this sort are rare, the disobedient acts usually causing no direct injury to persons or property, and imposing direct costs of a relatively minor kind and degree. If the correction of a serious injustice were indeed advanced by his protest, such immediate and obvious bad consequences might be often outweighed by the good accomplished. This does not complete the weighing, however. What the civil disobedient fails to appreciate is that his act does injury to the society of an intangible but specially serious kind. It breaks down respect for law in the community. By deliberately, knowingly, and publicly violating the law to further some specific political or social objectives, the civil disobedient—often a respected member of the community—sets the worst of examples, especially to the young.

Every well-ordered community is governed by laws, not men. Such government supposes not only the universal obligation to obey the laws, but also that this obligation is universally honored, and that the laws are generally respected. The duty to honor and respect the laws falls especially upon admired and well-educated citizens. When such citizens, whatever their moral fervor, take it upon themselves to break the law deliberately, whatever other consequences they may have in view, they help, through such conduct, to deteriorate the fabric of a law-abiding society. This fabric, so slowly and painfully woven, is the most treasured possession of a civilized community; what injures it is deeply pernicious. Because civil disobedience does injure that fabric, the evil it does can never be outweighed by the good it can accomplish.

This is a serious argument and deserves careful attention. In focusing not on the principles invoked in defending civil disobedience but on the act of disobedience itself, and its consequences, it demands some response from the disobedient. He, like his critic, avers a deep concern for the welfare of the society, and each of the two parties is prepared to defend his position as the one most likely to have the best consequences (or the fewest bad consequences) for that welfare.

The major premise of this social-fabric argument—that civilized community life depends upon respect for law and for the duly constituted authorities—may be accepted without qualms. Whether or not this respect for law is the very highest of civic virtues, it is of great importance, and we may readily grant that what injures it is indeed a threat to the well-being of the community.

It is possible, of course, that the wrong against which the civil disobedient protests is more serious than the alleged deleterious consequences to the social fabric. But even if it were, if his disobedience has the deteriorating consequences claimed it could be justifiable (within a utilitarian framework) only if the good the disobedience actually accomplishes in correcting that more serious evil outweighs such deterioration. Against the evil flowing from the disobedient act (if there is any) we must weigh not the good it was intended to accomplish but the good it does accomplish or, when that is impossible, the good it is likely to accomplish and the degree of that likelihood. But the destructive consequences of civil disobedience for the social fabric, if they ensue at all, ensue in good measure as a direct result of the deliberate disobedience of law; the good such protest accomplishes, in helping to correct some community injustice, is most often indirect and unsure. Therefore, if the breakdown of the respect for law does result from civil disobedience, such disobedience would be very difficult to justify on utilitarian grounds.

But does civil disobedience always cause, or tend to cause, disrespect for law and proper authority, or the breakdown of social order, or the general deterioration of the social fabric? The issue here is essentially factual, not philosophical, but the facts involved are exceedingly complex and difficult to determine accurately. Without careful and prolonged sociological studies to rely upon, all that can be done to resolve the issue is to examine generally communities in which civil disobedience has been practiced, trying to determine whether it did in fact result in the social deterioration this argument supposes. The evidence available from the American experience of the 1950s and 1960s does not seem to support the allegation.

It is true that there have been riots in the ghettos of some of our cities, and that many of the rioters have been inarticulately seeking redress of the same grievances against which civil disobedients sometimes protest. And it is true that civil disobedience has sometimes been practiced in the same cities in which civil riots have later taken place. But this concatenation certainly does not prove, or even tend to show, that the one is the cause of the other. That both civil disobedience and social disorders arise in the same communities is no accident, of course. They are both reactions to grave social problems, being entirely different ways of attacking these problems. Their fundamental natures, however, are utterly opposed, the spirit in which they are undertaken quite contrasting, and the persons who pursue them usually quite distinct. (See Chapter II, Section 4.) It is naïve to suppose that civil disobedience is the cause of civil riots; more than naïve, it is dangerous as well. For in placing the blame on "irresponsible demonstrators," we obscure the real faults of an irresponsive public; in denouncing "agitators" (usually supposed to come from somewhere else) who allegedly deteriorate the social fabric, we blind ourselves to the real causes of social disorder and then misdirect our corrective efforts, inviting disorders of ever greater magnitude.

These two, disparate social phenomena require much careful study if we are to understand well their causes and their consequences. But on the surface, at least, the correlation between them has been, in view of the social tensions present, surprisingly low. In most cases civil disobedience has been practiced in smaller communities and cities in which riot has neither threatened nor ensued. In most such communities it has had no tendency whatever to promote disorder or disrespect. Where the object of the disobedient protest is some injustice whose victims are distant from the locus of the protest, the disobedience itself has no tendency to encourage a generalized disobedience or defiance of the laws. On the other hand, in those cities in which massive disorders have taken place, civil disobedience has seldom been practiced before them, and almost never by the same persons or under the same leadership or in the same places in which the riots developed. If there is a real link between the two, it is not a causal one, nor is it the mere fact that both are illegal (since in the one case the law-breaking is incidental to the generalized passion). Rather, this link may be the deep social discontent that underlies them both. In view of the generality of that discontent they remain remarkably distinct and arise as wholly different reactions to it, almost as though from two different worlds.

Rampant lawlessness and violence are understandably a source of great distress and anxiety for the decent citizen. But in seeking to put an end to them it is foolish for him to grasp at straws. Every citizen, in the absence of more scientific reports, must form his own judgment concerning what the actual consequences of civil disobedience have been. As a resident and an observer of a municipality in which civil disobedience has been several times employed in recent years, I would report that so far as I can tell, its practice has had little or no tendency to encourage disrespect for law or to cause a general deterioration of the social order.

Quite the reverse seems commonly true, in fact. The preservation of an atmosphere in which the laws are taken seriously and respected is a most important value, and the controlled and thoughtful practice of civil disobedience does more to support that value than to defeat it. This, for several reasons. First, because the civil disobedient breaks the law *and is punished,* and his punishment follows his crime with sureness and with much public attention. Others may follow his example in rendering strong protest, but not as a lark. Having one's self arrested, tried, punished (with all the incidental opportunities for maltreatment) is hardly anybody's idea of good fun. Second, because the civil disobedient (justified or not) has an evident solicitude for the justice of the laws, even if his act is believed too extreme, a significant portion of the community is likely to reflect upon the alleged injustice. In making the justice or injustice of the laws a matter of greater public concern, civil disobedience has a beneficial effect, not an adverse one, upon the general social atmosphere. Third, quite apart from the particular object of the disobedient's protest, or the evaluation of that protest, his act has the effect of turning community attention toward the laws in general—their content, their enforcement, their universal importance. Good laws, general obedience to them, and fair enforcement of them, are central values for a democratic community—and yet serious malfunctions of the legal system are not rare. Sometimes these malfunctions are due to the deliberate efforts of persons or parties; more often they are the result of ignorance or mistake on the part of legislators or law-enforcement agencies. In either case, if a real injustice is allowed to continue in a genuine democracy, it must be receiving indirect public support, through public neglect. Correction of such malfunctions, therefore, is most surely fostered through the general attentiveness of the citizenry to the character and operation of its legal system. This attentiveness, both formal and informal, is invariably increased—perhaps slightly, perhaps markedly—by the intelligent practice of civil disobedience. By helping to create and sustain a widespread *interest* in the laws, the civil disobedient does more than most men ever do to support the general respect for them that well-ordered communities require.

Yet another factor ought to be kept in mind. The enforcement of laws that are widely believed to be unjust, or are very unpopular for other reasons, may do much more to engender disrespect for law in general than would deliberate disobedience under some circumstances. Misbehavior on the part of law-making or law-enforcing authorities—negligence, or insensitivity, or corruption—truly rots the social fabric. Such misbehavior, all too frequent, deserves strong critical response. Sometimes disobedience is the only effective response available. In such extraordinary cases respect for law may suffer more from compliance than from noncompliance.

This much, however, can be granted to one who presents the social-fabric argument: *if* the net result of civil disobedience really is the deteriorating effect upon community respect for law and order alleged, *then* it is unlikely that any case of indirect civil disobedience, at least, could be justified. But the antecedent of this hypothetical proposition is very probably false.

Even were that antecedent shown true in some circumstances, moreover, the justifiability of *direct* civil disobedience would remain to be determined. For it would remain possible that the long-range consequences of obedience to some grossly unjust command would be far worse for all concerned than deliberate disobedience of the commanding authority, with whatever disrespect for authority that disobedience might engender.

6. FIFTH ARGUMENT:
Civil Disobedience Is Self-Defeating

The practice of civil disobedience defeats its own purposes. Even when its objectives are worthy, the deliberate unlawfulness it involves creates, in the minds of both legislators and general public, a widespread feeling of resentment and anger. By making enemies rather than friends, and by offending innocent bystanders, the civil disobedient produces an adverse reaction to his cause, and undermines thereby his own larger objectives. Civil disobedience cannot be justified, therefore, by the claimed advancement of worthy goals, since its ultimate effect is not their achievement but the retardation of that very advance.

This, too, is a serious argument, and one to which the civil disobedient must respond, since it is certainly true that resentment and anger are sometimes produced by disobedient (and often even by wholly lawful) protest demonstrations. It must be granted immediately that in some circumstances civil disobedience is (whatever else we may say about it) tactically unwise, a mistake from the point of view of the protesters themselves, although it is understandable that they should later find it difficult to admit this, even to themselves.

On the other side it should be realized that in allowing certain kinds of community injustice to develop and to become ingrained in the society, all citizens must share the blame. If the community is a reasonably democratic one, this blameworthiness of the ordinary citizen is not insignificant. When disobedient protests against racial discrimination, or an unjust war, seem offensive in the eyes of the many citizens, it is not mainly "innocent bystanders" who are thus offended. Leaders of the civil rights movement in America put this very well: on some issues you are either not a bystander, or you are not innocent.

Granting this, the force of this utilitarian argument against civil disobedience—that it defeats its own purposes—remains uncertain. Whether the argument succeeds depends upon the particular context both of the grievance and of the protest, and the issue can be decided fairly only when that background is very well understood. Even with such understanding, the argument's force depends upon certain factual claims about the consequences of the disobedient act that are very difficult to assess.

Whether civil disobedience creates serious resentment or anger in a given case, and has the long-range adverse impact claimed, depends at least upon: (a) the immediate and foreseeable consequences of that disobedient act; (b) the object of protest; (c) the intrinsic nature of the disobedient act; and (d) the relation of that act to the object of protest. In each of these dimensions the possibilities lie along a roughly determinable continuum.

Where the immediate consequences of the disobedient act involve no injury to property, and only minor inconvenience, if any, to anyone other than the protesters themselves—as in the case of a carefully organized, and peaceful, unlawful sit-in—general irritation should be minimized, and an angry reaction by many is unlikely. Where the consequences of the disobedient act involve some considerable inconvenience to the community, or even clear harm to it—as when traffic is badly blocked, or military preparations interfered with—the likelihood of resentment and adverse reaction increases, of course. But minimizing inconvenience for others is no guarantee that resentment will not be severe. Some forms of civil disobedience—the public destruction of one's draft card, or the public desecration of the flag—cause direct inconvenience for virtually no one but the disobedient himself and yet may provoke an almost wild response. Destruction of one's draft card has no effect upon his eligibility for induction, or upon administrative process, but this act sometimes arouses the most bitter animosity in persons not themselves subject to induction. The showing of disrespect for the flag by a single person or small minority has no significant effect upon anybody, but it can be severely punished by law and will drive some patriots into a rage. Acts of protest, especially when disobedient, can offend by their symbolic impact as well as by their practical consequences. If the substantive issue is controversial, as it often is, the act that is harmless but symbolically necessary in the eyes of the protester may be dishonorable and symbolically offensive in the eyes of much of his audience. Of course symbolic impact may be one of the protester's deliberate instruments; but he must weigh very carefully the consequences of the use of that instrument if he hopes his act to be effective, and justifiable.

Where the object of protest is some clearly unjust inequality of treatment—as in most civil rights demonstrations in the United States—the onlooker is likely to feel some empathy with the protester, and irritation created by deliberate disobedience will be mitigated by his justifiable feelings of self-guilt for supporting the system that provokes that disobedience. Where the object of protest is some political decision or administrative act whose wisdom is arguable, and which, however mistaken in fact, is the result of a careful judgment by duly constituted authorities, resentment against disobedient protest is likely to be stronger, unmitigated by any feelings of guilt on the part of ordinary citizens, and more likely to spur opposition to the protester's conduct and cause.

Where the disobedient act is, in itself, a minor violation of law—say, a trespass or some minor traffic infraction—resentment (if any) is likely to be weakly felt and short-lived. Where the disobedient act is, in itself, a serious violation of a law whose burdens are borne widely—say, refusal to be inducted, or refusal to pay one's taxes—the resentment felt by those who also face those legal duties, and fulfill them, is understandably likely to be more bitter and more long-lasting.

Whether the disobedience is direct or indirect is likely to have considerable bearing upon the reaction with which it is met. Direct disobedience will be more readily and more fully understood, even by those not in full sympathy with the protest. Where the disobedience is direct, the infraction minor, and its consequences involve little or no injury to the community—the historic "freedom rides" and the lunch counter "sit-ins" in the American South are outstanding examples—the general reaction of the community is likely to be one of consternation and reflection, and the probability of success in achieving a worthy objective is reasonably high. Unfortunately, when the disobedience is to be direct it is also true that the protester loses much control over the precise character of his protest and its consequences. The gravity of the crime and its possible punishment must depend upon the law that is directly disobeyed, and the disobedient obviously has no control over the passage or the formulation of that law. He may not be able to select the circumstances of his disobedience, or even the form that it will take. Through all of this he must hope that the principled nature of his violation will be generally understood, its essence as protest appreciated. This again is more likely to happen if no private benefit accrues from the disobedient act or, if there is private benefit, the person benefitted is not the disobedient himself. When the benefit appears to accrue to the disobedient himself (as in cases of draft refusal, tax refusal, and the like), the chances of misunderstanding and adverse reaction sharply increase. This remains true, even though the ensuing penalty will greatly outweigh the immediate private gain. (See this chapter, Section 3.)

Indirect disobedience gives to the protester far greater control over the nature, the timing, and the general circumstances of his disobedient act. Through the intelligent exercise of this control he may hope to hold adverse reaction to a minimum, although he is unlikely ever to eliminate it entirely. His great handicap in this sphere is the additional burden of explaining his protest, or seeing that it gets explained fairly, to a public likely to be apathetic and inattentive. Somehow he must make it clear—if adverse reaction is to be minimized —that he breaks one law to protest something else, an injustice he cannot attack more directly. It may not be a very complicated message, but the protester must expect that large numbers of voting citizens are either not going to receive that message at all, or will get it in so garbled a form that they will be ill-disposed to side with him.

This handicap, added to the natural inclination of law-abiding citizens to view any deliberate disobedience with a jaundiced eye, makes it especially crucial that the indirect civil disobedient choose the form and circumstances of his disobedient act with intelligence and care. Several practical considerations must be weighed by him in making that choice.

First in importance, when the disobedience is indirect, is that the act be minimally harmful to persons or property of the community. Deliberate destruction, even if minor, or deliberate invitations to disorder (even if the protesters themselves are orderly) will be rightly resented and may create so much opposition to a worthy cause as to be simply unjustifiable. There is no single form that indirect disobedience must invariably take, but its form should be such as to expose the protester to punishment while injuring or inconveniencing the community little if at all. A certain amount of expense to the community, in consuming the time of law-enforcement officers, courts, and the like, is unavoidable. Ideally, these expenses too will be minimized by advising authorities (when feasible) of the time and place of the planned disobedient protest, and by the protesters' cooperation with law-enforcement officers in effecting their own arrest.

Second in importance is clarity of communication to the general public of the aims of and reasons for the disobedient protest. The handicap previously described has got to be overcome. This is likely to require considerable planning and organizational effort, as well as good public relations work. Indirect disobedience without adequate public explanation is most unlikely to be either effective or justifiable. A serious message has got to be disseminated in a large, preoccupied, and partly hostile community; how well or how poorly that message gets through will greatly affect the generality and intensity of supporting and adverse reactions. Whether the protest undermines its own objectives, therefore, may vitally depend upon how much preparation has gone into it.

Beyond these two considerations, the form of protest must be visible and efficacious without being offensive; the message must not only be clear but loud. To this end, ingenuity is necessary in selecting the date and the place of the disobedient act, and in choosing an appropriately open and dramatic form for the protest. Precise timing, the personal manner and dress of the protesters, their public utterances during and after the protest—all these and similar factors will affect the reactions among the public for whom the protest is undertaken.

Even with the most careful attention to factors of this sort, the indirect civil disobedient is never going to be a popular fellow; his deliberate law-breaking is not going to be greeted with public acclaim. But his object is to accomplish some worthy social objective, and if he is really sincere in this he must strive to reduce the animosities that would hinder the accomplishment of that objective. In some cases the adverse reactions to his protest will be so intense as to outweigh the good he does; the disobedience then is not justifiable. But in other cases those adverse reactions can and may be minimized, and are themselves outweighed by the effectiveness of the protest. Whether any particular indirect disobedient protest achieves this desired reaction depends upon the facts of that case, upon how successful that protester is in choosing a disobedient act that is minimally harmful and circumstances that are maximally public—while making widely and vividly clear the honorable object of his protest.

Finally, the claim that civil disobedience defeats its own purposes must be examined with a clear understanding of what the disobedient hopes to accomplish directly through his act. He does not normally expect the immediate enactment of the change he seeks. His strategy is not one aimed at making friends, or causing people to like or admire him, and thereby coaxing them into giving their political support. His track is an entirely different one. His immediate object is to force public attention to what should be a grave concern of the community. That object he may accomplish regardless of the ensuing attitudes of the public toward him, and even a wave of resentment may do more to waken general social consciousness than anything else he can do. He may reason, perhaps correctly, that the only hope for a long-term remedy is community action arising out of reflection, and that he must try to sting the body politic into that reflective state. Moreover, the civil disobedient may further his long-range objectives even while becoming himself despised (and perhaps giving his enemies a short-term political weapon) if, in so doing, he also forces his opponents to acknowledge their support of a social injustice. The disobedient cannot by himself effect the desired change. But he may succeed in exposing the need for that change and in identifying those who seek to block it. That done, he may rely upon the conscience of the community at large, suffering quietly the ridicule and harassment that may befall him as a result of his efforts to stir that conscience.

7. SIXTH ARGUMENT:

Lawlessness Cannot Be Justified When Lawful Channels Remain Open

Although civil disobedience may sometimes prove justifiable under arbitrary or dictatorial rule, it can never be justified under a constitutional government within which there exist lawful channels for the registering of protest, and lawful means for the correction of the wrong protested.

This is a bad argument, although it is often heard. Its plausibility arises from the conviction that where there are two ways of achieving the same objective, one lawful and the other not, the unlawful procedure (other things being equal) would not be justifiable. This principle is entirely reasonable, and every civil disobedient may accept it. But taken by itself it does not support the argument at hand, because it does not apply to many circumstances in which civil disobedience is practiced. Other things are often not equal, and the problem is rarely so simple as that of choosing between a lawful and an unlawful course of equivalent effectiveness. The point is that lawful channels may exist on paper but not in fact; or they may be real but quite unusable in the existing circumstances. Even if there are lawful channels for the registering of protest, it does not follow that using them will be (or could be) as effective as the far more dramatic protest of the civil disobedient. Showing that lawful protest is possible, therefore, cannot by itself prove that disobedient protest is unjustifiable; what would have to be shown is that (assuming the object of protest is a wrong badly in need of remedy) some practical form of legal protest would be equally (or almost equally) effective in accomplishing the much

Case 15. *The New York Times (21 January 1968) carried a letter from a staff member of the organization known as the Resistance, presenting another version of the reply to this argument. The letter reads in part:*

Your January 18 editorial suggests that opposition to the draft would have done better to seek reform and redress within what you refer to as the "normal machinery of a democratic society." This of course implies that effective legal channels of meaningful political and social change still exist—or have ever existed—within the United States.

It is true, and certainly easy enough for you to write, that contemporary America is not Nazi Germany; the methods of control our Government employs are infinitely more subtle and sophisticated. Only on infrequent occasions—such as we witnessed in Detroit last summer—is it necessary for those in power to resort to naked violence.

Even the firmest believer in American democracy must admit there is an inconsistency in demanding that the Government's rules be adhered to by an eighteen, nineteen or twenty-year-old man who is included in the Selective Service system but excluded from voting in all but a handful of states.

Furthermore, while it may be possible that legal protest and political action can in time bring about a reversal of United States military policy, the urgency of the Vietnam war demands a response which simultaneously forces the American public to face

needed change. But that cannot always be shown because, in some circumstances at least, disobedient protest has a moral force and public effectiveness that lawful protest cannot match.

Similarly, it is little consolation to those who suffer from oppression or injustice (or to those who are deeply pained by the unjust suffering of others) to know that there exist constitutional channels through which remedies might some-the gravity of our crimes (skeptics should read Frank Harvey's *Air War Vietnam*) in Asia and sets into motion a process for ending the war. Draft resistance is just such a response.

The undeniable fact that we resisters face heavy penalties for our open actions of refusal to register for the draft, to carry draft cards and to be inducted, lends a seriousness to our arguments which cannot be overlooked.

Our violations of the Selective Service law are a plea to America's conscience to consider not only the five years' imprisonment we face, but also to consider the constant threat the Vietnamese people face daily under the shadow of U.S. bombers.

At the same time the draft resistance movement creates a community of concern beyond the individual resistant. His heretofore apathetic relatives are now alarmed that a member of their family is likely to be jailed. Waves in the society are created which lead to growing (albeit unarticulated) anti-war sentiment. Whatever quasi-democratic institutions exist in America become to some extent responsive to such popular discontent. In this way a latent function of our civil disobedience is to reinforce and complement legal political activities.

Finally, resistance to the draft dramatizes the moral confrontation with Selective Service in a manner that no legal protest can achieve. . . ."

(Signed) Stephen Suffet
Draft Card Burner

day come. The civil disobedient is often moved to his protest just because, with these channels present and acknowledged, the remedies do not come—and do not even appear likely. Civil disobedience is a tactic resorted to when the normal processes of politics fail to meet the most pressing needs of some segment of the community, needs that could and should be met. It is a form of protest designed to do what normal political activities have not done and do not appear likely to succeed in doing. It is true that real costs, both personal and social, are imposed by this disobedience. But that these costs, because they include deliberate infractions of the law, must necessarily outweigh the gains in long-term social justice is precisely what the civil disobedient, after careful reflection, denies. His assessment of the pros and cons in any given case may be mistaken; but to assume that the mere *possibility* of lawful remedy necessarily refutes the case of the civil disobedient is to exhibit a failure to understand that case and begs the central question. (See Case 15, pp. 164–65.)

Those who present this argument sometimes have in mind a rather different claim, one that is both weaker and more reasonable. They may be saying, in effect:

If vigorous efforts to achieve the desired remedy through normal political channels have not been persistently pursued, or if vigorous lawful protests (even of an abnormal kind) have not been made against the failure to effect such remedy, then the resort to unlawful protest is likely to be unjustifiable. For in the absence of such efforts there can be no assurance that disobedience was a necessary recourse, that other means, less costly and more orderly, might not have had similar, or even better results.

This is a conditional claim (if P then Q) and is entirely reasonable taken as a whole. But having accepted it as a whole, the consequent (Q—that disobedience is not justifiable) cannot be generally inferred, because the antecedent (P—that lawful protest has not been vigorously pursued) does not accord with the facts of most actual cases. Many (probably most) who practice civil disobedience do so only after long-continued political activity of every reasonable sort in pursuit of the same objectives. Agitation within political parties, organized lobbying, personal campaigning—every sort of legitimate political practice is likely to have been tried at length and to have proved ineffective. Moreover, lawful protests against inaction, in most cases, will have been registered repeatedly, in a great variety of ways, from the more normal letters of protest to representatives and editors, and petitions for action, to the less common (but still lawful) marches of protest, vigils of protest, and public assemblies of prayer and protest. It is when all these have failed that civil disobedience gets serious consideration as an alternative. Of course it will not be easy to determine, in a given case, whether the normal political processes have been fully enough explored, or when lawful channels of protest have been exhausted and proved ineffective. But in exceptional cases they may have been, whereupon exceptional tactics—even deliberate disobedience—may prove justifiable.

8. SEVENTH ARGUMENT:

Civil Disobedience Cannot Be Justified Because It Subverts Democratic Process

Civil disobedience is never justifiable in a reasonably healthy democratic community. It is unjustifiable not simply because it breaks the law, but because in breaking the law deliberately it violates the procedural rules that an operating democracy presupposes. These rules, which set limits on the manner in which participants may seek to influence community decision-making, are the foundation of a just government. Therefore, when they are deliberately disregarded or defied the loss is profound, greater by far than whatever good might flow from effective protest against one substantive evil. Indeed, although the civil disobedient claims to act within the frame of the legal system, his act is, in effect, a deep form of revolution, procedural if not substantive.

He subverts the entire game, by deliberately breaking its rules. He applies a form of pressure illegitimate in the political arena, thereby vitiating (to the extent he is effective) the principle of majority rule. He creates, in effect, a state of war between himself and his community, forcing the community to respond similarly, subverting and rendering inapplicable the democratic process that, in whole, is far more to be prized than any particular substantive goal.

This argument goes deep. Although it bears a superficial resemblance to the preceding argument in attending to normal political process, it is in fact fundamentally different. This argument does not claim that a protest made through normal channels can be as effective as civil disobedience, or that the same results can be achieved. Rather, it suggests that however inadequate the citizen may find the normal channels of democratic political action in achieving a given end, those inadequacies do not justify the abandonment and subversion of the system. I do not think this argument is sound, but if there is any one argument that can serve to show civil disobedience to be always unjustifiable in a healthy democracy, this one (or some variant of it) is likely to be it.

Two lines of reply are open, either or both of which could defeat the argument as it is applied to at least some (perhaps many) instances of civil disobedience.

The first reply denies the premise that is the core of the argument: that civil disobedience does subvert, or tend to subvert, the political process of a healthy democracy. That subversion is held to result from the deliberate disregard of the ground-rules of the political game. Suppose it agreed that an operating democracy does presuppose a set of rules laying down permissible patterns of participation. Important questions about these rules would remain to be answered. The key question for the present purpose is whether such rules forbid all cases of controlled disobedience as a form of participation in the decision-making process. Allowing that there are such uncodified but generally accepted rules, there would probably be much dispute over precisely what they permit or forbid. Merely to assert, as this argument does, that civil disobedience necessarily violates these fundamental rules is, again, to beg the crucial question.

It is probably impossible to prove that, if democracy does presuppose some set of ground-rules, civil disobedience does not necessarily violate them. But it is not hard to see the main reason many are led to think that it must violate them. That reason is simply the general conviction that, whatever else a healthy polity must be, it must be *law-governed*, and that therefore no conduct that is deliberately unlawful can be within the rules. There is a non sequitur here however. A healthy polity must indeed be governed by laws, but that requirement does not prove that deliberate disobedience of some of these laws must, under any circumstances, subvert the system of government. At least in some cases the disobedience may be of such a nature, be undertaken under such carefully controlled circumstances, and be met with such clear and immediate punishment, that its upshot is more the reinforcement than the weakening of the law-governed character of the polity. As in the fourth argument above (Section 5), but now on a deeper level, the critic bases his attack on the supposition that civil disobedience necessarily repudiates or weakens (or seeks to repudiate or weaken) legitimate authority, while in fact it generally does neither.

The critic may rejoin:

This reply does not meet the full thrust of my argument. I maintain not merely that civil disobedience upsets a government of laws but that it disrupts the orderly, non-violent process through which laws come to be formulated and adopted. The point is that democratic decision-making is properly the outcome of pushes and pulls by participating interest groups, and there have got to be rules about how hard one may push. Some pushes are so vigorous that they throw the whole process out of kilter. Civil disobedience is of that kind. It makes the orderly continuation of a bargaining, compromising process difficult or impossible. It functions as a kind of threat, a political blackjack, which forces the opponents either to knuckle under or to resort to devices equally threatening and disruptive, thereby leading to the progressive degeneration of effective democratic process.

This claim appears plausible, but it is probably not accurate. What is before us is another of those hard factual questions about the operation of democracy to which it is impossible to give answers with universal applicability. Deliberate violation of some laws—say, election laws—may adversely affect the entire democratic process. Other laws may be broken without having any effect upon the entire system, and certainly without undermining it. One who deliberately trespasses on a military base to protest, say, the testing of a nuclear weapon on that base, and submits readily to arrest and punishment, having publicly announced the plans for his protest in advance, may indeed be exerting a real pressure on the public and the legislature. He pretty well forces them to hear his objections; but he pays a very high price for his audience, and he is very unlikely to get his own way, nor is he likely to disrupt in any way the process by which laws are adopted—either the laws governing military authorities or the laws concerning trespass. His push is no more disruptive than that of an influential publisher who uses the news columns of his paper to editorialize vigorously on behalf of one candidate in an election, or the push of a legislator who, in the effort to combat what he believes to be oppressive legislation, filibusters against it. We may be pained by the unbalanced coverage of the editor, and by the disruptive tactics of the legislator, but we do not deny that their conduct is, even if offensive to some, within the rules of the political process. If there is impropriety in such conduct we seek to make that impropriety redound to the disadvantage of its authors. Similarly, we may be pained by the pressures exerted by the civil disobedient (especially if the substance of his complaint is not to our liking), and we may honor and respond more cooperatively to a protest that does not incorporate deliberate disobedience. But that does not show the disobedient to have employed a pernicious or subversive tactic. He sacrifices himself, not the laws; whereas many whom we admit (perhaps reluctantly) are playing the game sacrifice community well-being in the quest for private gain. The claim that every case of civil disobedience violates the fundamental procedural principles of democracy, or subverts the rule of the majority, simply cannot be substantiated.

A second line of defense against this argument, supposing—what ought not be granted—that civil disobedience does tend to subvert democratic process, questions the conclusion then drawn from this premise. This subversion is an evil so great, we may allow, that if indeed it is the consequence of every case of civil disobedience the great majority of such protests will not be justifiable. But it does not follow that such protests will *never* be justifiable. It is surely conceivable that some acts of civil disobedience, particularly direct disobedience, may be aimed at laws or policies so cruel and unjust (although enacted democratically) that the good done by the disobedience outweighs the evil done (if it is done) in disrupting the democracy. This might be the case, for example, when a citizen refuses a lawful order to kill, or when he deliberately and unlawfully obstructs the development of an horrendous weapon system. Allowing that the maintenance of healthy democratic process is a very high value indeed, we need not agree that its maximization takes moral priority over all other considerations.

The task of successfully defending an act of civil disobedience is never easy. If no one of the arguments discussed above can demolish every such defense, it remains possible that no single instance of civil disobedience can escape them all. So it is necessary, in order to show that a given case of civil disobedience is in fact justifiable, that it be defended against all of these arguments, and perhaps others. I have deliberately refrained from attempting to provide such a defense, even of an ideal case, because to do so properly would require the most thorough elaboration of the circumstances, past and present, of the instance chosen. Such an elaboration is inappropriate, as well as impossible, here.

I do not pretend to have examined every possible argument against the practice of civil disobedience or to have said the last word on any one of those I have discussed. But I do think that the main lines of the major arguments concerning it have been dealt with here. None of them succeeds in showing that civil disobedience can never be justified.

⋖§ VII §⋗

CIVIL DISOBEDIENCE AND
FREE SPEECH

1. THE PROBLEM

What has civil disobedience to do with the freedom of speech? The one is a device to which a few resort under very exceptional circumstances, the other a basic principle of democratic government applying to all citizens in virtually all circumstances. Yet some disobedients have argued that the link between these two concepts is of vital importance in understanding their acts. This claim must be examined.

The concern here is not merely with special cases in which the object of a disobedient's protest is some restriction of free speech. Such cases are infrequent and raise no theoretical problem about civil disobedience that has not already been introduced. Rather, what must be examined is the argument sometimes—but only rarely—raised by civil disobedients to this effect: their disobedient act is itself a form of political speech, even though a deliberate infraction of some statute, and therefore must be protected by constitutional provisions that protect every man's right to express himself openly and forcefully on subjects of community concern. In its specially

✑ *Case 16. An orderly and wholly nonviolent protest against the war in Vietnam was conducted on 15 October 1965 in Ann Arbor, Michigan, by a group of students at The University of Michigan. They marched with placards urging the end of the war and maintained a peaceful picket line at the office building in which the local draft board was located. A number of the protesters then entered the building, proceeded to the office of the board, and occupied the public portion of that office by sitting upon the available chairs and upon the floor as a continuing part of the protest demonstration of the day. At the close of the board's business day they were asked to leave the premises. They refused to do so and were arrested as violators of the Michigan trespass statute; they were convicted in municipal court. Appealing that conviction to the Washtenaw County Circuit Court (CR File No. 951, October 1965), the preliminary statement in the brief filed by their attorneys read, in part:*

The defendants are charged with what appears to be a minor offense—trespass on property. Yet the issues raised by their defense are as important as any which have been litigated in the

American variant, the argument claims that civil disobedience in which local or state laws have been violated cannot be lawfully punished in view of the provisions of the First Amendment to the *Constitution of the United States*, which reads in part: "Congress shall make no law . . . abridging the freedom of speech. . . ." (See Case 16.)

This argument adopts a peculiar position on the question of the justification of the disobedient act and is importantly different from the patterns of justification previously discussed. Its foundation is neither purely legal nor purely moral. On the one hand, he who presents this argument does not seek to give a legal justification for the disobedient act by showing that, in some larger legal context, his act broke no course of American jurisprudence. For what is involved in the defense is the nature and extent of the right or duty of a citizen of a nation to protest the actions of his own government which he considers to be in violation of International law and morality.

In this brief we will endeavor to present rational argument and legal justification for the proposition that the "sit-in" as a form of non-violent civil protest under the circumstances of this case, is an appropriate means for effectively communicating sincerely-held views on a vital political issue and should be protected under the First Amendment.

On this and other grounds the case was ably argued; but the appeal failed, and the defendants received sentences (for trespass violations) ranging from fifteen to twenty days in jail, plus fines of $50 each. Once again they appealed their conviction, now to the Michigan Court of Appeals (Mich. App. 709, 1966). In the new brief submitted in their behalf appeared the following argument:

It is significant that no attempt was made by the police or draft board authorities to cause defendants' arrest or eviction for disturbance of the peace, trespass, or any other violation of local

law. He does not maintain that the statute violated was itself unconstitutional, or that it was being used as subterfuge to accomplish unconstitutional objectives, and that therefore he disobeyed no valid statute. Such an argument (see Chapter V, Section 2) essentially denies that the act in question was disobedient and seeks a justification of the conduct on wholly legal grounds. In the argument now before us the disobedient admits that his act was a violation of a statute and that the law broken was a perfectly valid one that he has no desire to question. Even so, he argues, he must not be punished under it because of a constitutional provision that permits even deliberate disobedience of such laws when undertaken with certain clear ends in view—namely, the public expression of *or state law until some time following the official hour of closing the office. Even then, the arrest of the defendants was not initiated by the law enforcement authorities, but by the Selective Service, the occupant of the office.*

Thus, it is clear that defendants' conduct in this case in sitting-in at the draft board offices and remaining there for several hours was accepted by the local and draft board authorities as a legitimate, albeit annoying, method of expressing their opposition to the Government's Vietnam policies.

Thus, this case represents the classic example of the "expression" character of a sit-in protest, as distinguished from those cases where the form of protest was violative of public order or where injury to the private property rights of others was intended. Defendants offered to prove that on the day prior to the protest, the City Administrator held a meeting in his office with the Episcopal Chaplain at the University, the director of a campus religious organization, a university professor and one of the defendants who was a leader of the protest, to lay the ground rules for the sit-in, so as to avoid any public disturbance or unnecessary difficulties for the police and the defendants.

important political ideas. This argument is not purely moral in character either; it is partly a legal argument insofar as it relies ultimately upon the provisions of the constitution of the community (in this case, the United States) and the guarantees there provided to all citizens. At the same time it does not deny the illegality, on another level, of the act performed.

The argument is peculiar in a second sense. Any civil disobedient who presents it in his own defense clearly departs from the normal practice of this form of protest (see Chapter IV, Section 3), which calls for an admission of technical guilt and a public readiness to pay the penalty of deliberate

The community thus recognized the sincerity of the protestants, the importance of the public issue involved in the protest and its symbolic character; on the other hand the defendants acknowledged the authority of the police to arrest. Implicit in the conduct and attitude of both parties was the assumption that the Court would ultimately determine whether, under the circumstances, the trespass law or the First Amendment would govern.

The Trial Judge excluded this evidence as immaterial. We believe that in so ruling he erred, for the evidence would tend to support defendants' contention that their protest was a form of expression protected by the First Amendment. It was also relevant to the question of intent or wilfulness, a matter discussed later in this brief.

Within the context of the relevant Supreme Court decisions, the peaceful, public protest by these university students and faculty members upon an important public issue must be evaluated by this Court as a form of expression to be measured against the property right asserted, by the exacting standards required by the First Amendment.

Again they lost their appeal.

infraction as one way of prodding the conscience of the community. I return to that aspect of the matter shortly.

I shall try to present this argument as persuasively as I can; but I conclude in the end that it does not stand up under careful scrutiny.

2. THE ARGUMENT

We begin with the supposition, never in question here, that there is a pressing and permanent need for the strong and active protection of free expression of every kind. Especially in the political sphere, and most especially when the issues are highly controversial, speech must be completely free and protected or democracy cannot thrive. The constitution of the community—whether written or unwritten—must be the guarantee of that freedom. Let us suppose all that agreed upon.

The present issue, then, is one of determining how far the protection of free speech really goes. The proponent of the present argument—call him Z—wishes only to maintain that the defense of civil disobedients is a natural and appropriate application of constitutional protections of free speech.

Speech, after all, is an elastic and generic term. What is called speech may take a great variety of forms, of which actual talking and writing are only two of the most obvious. Whatever the form, the essential element in speech activity (Z argues) is the effort to communicate ideas. Gestures, symbolic responses, certain conventional patterns of conduct, and a variety of other nonverbal acts often accomplish such communication, as they are designed to do. This extension of speech to nonverbal acts is not merely a flight of fancy but an established practice of the highest courts. One relevant example is the technique of picketing in a labor dispute, long punished as a violation of state laws in the United States. In 1940 the United States Supreme Court, in a decision most would now applaud (*Thornhill v. Alabama,* 310 U.S. 88, 1940), declared such picketing worthy of protection under the freedom of speech provisions of the First Amendment. Now picketing consists for the most part of physical acts, but taken in context its aim is clearly to get a message across to potential workers or customers of the firm picketed. Similarly, in a whole series of cases in the 1960s concerning public protest demonstrations against racial discrimination, convictions for the alleged violation of state trespass statutes and the like were consistently reversed by the Supreme Court. A classic example is that of a Louisiana case involving blacks who sat waiting to be served at the white lunch counter of a segregated department store. They were arrested, charged with disturbance of the peace, tried, convicted, and sentenced to imprisonment and fine. After the Louisiana courts upheld the convictions, the U.S. Supreme Court reversed them unanimously. In addition to racial equality, issues of free speech were clearly involved. Justice Harlan, in a concurring opinion, held that there was much more to the apparently disobedient conduct of the Negroes in this case

than a bare desire to remain at the "white" lunch counter. . . . Such a demonstration . . . is as much a part of the "free trade in ideas" . . . as is verbal expression, more commonly thought of as "speech." It, like speech, appeals to good sense and to "the power of reason as applied through public discussion . . ." just as much as, if not more than, a public oration delivered from a soapbox at a street corner. This Court has never limited the right to speak . . . to mere verbal expression. [Garner v. Louisiana, 368 U.S. 157, 1961.]

The protection of free speech has been extended by the courts not only where the act in question (which functioned as speech) was forbidden by unconstitutional statutes or by statutes improperly maintaining racial discrimination in some form. Open and uninhibited political criticism is of such fundamental importance in a democracy that conduct that falls into this category will be protected even when it may appear to fall also into categories otherwise rightly unlawful. So, for example, what might otherwise be thought libel will sometimes be protected by constitutional guarantees. There is, the

U.S. Supreme Court said in 1964, "a proud national commitment to the principle that debate on public issues should be uninhibited, robust, and wide open, and that it may well include vehement, caustic, and sometimes unpleasantly sharp attacks on government and public officials." (*The New York Times Co. v. Sullivan*, 376 U.S. 254, 1964.) Apparently libelous attacks on public figures may, to that end (the Court went on) deserve protection. "Like insurrection, contempt, advocacy of unlawful acts, breach of the peace, obscenity, solicitation of legal business and the other various formulae . . . that have been challenged in this Court, libel cannot claim talismanic immunity from constitutional limitations." The point is clear: an act that deserves the protection of the Constitution because of its essential nature continues to deserve that protection even should it violate some statutes clearly within the power of legislatures to enact.

Why then should trespass, or other minor infractions obviously employed as forms of indirect civil disobedience, not be treated likewise? Calling an act a trespass (which we may take as a representative case), or a traffic violation, or a breach of the peace, does not remove it from First Amendment protection. The key question, according to Z, is whether a given deliberate violation of law truly functions as a form of political speech. In practice the issue will be arguable, of course, but it is one that reasonable men may decide fairly. If it is a form of speech it is surely entitled to the same constitutional protections afforded to all other political speech.

Of course real interests are safeguarded by state trespass and traffic laws and the like, and these are on the whole good laws. Z never questions that. But such interests must be balanced against the interests of the entire community in maximally free expression. The Supreme Court has repeatedly recognized the need, in similar situations, to balance the one set of interests against the other, and in this process always to give basic constitutional freedoms a considerable amount of "breathing space." In clear cases of indirect civil disobedience (Z's argument continues) such a balancing would surely result in the exculpation of a minor infraction, even if deliberate, provided it were carefully supervised and unambiguously intended as a political protest. The indirect civil disobedient, it will be remembered, normally chooses an act that minimizes public harm and inconvenience yet is performed under the public eye, with procedural details for the arrest of the protesters often arranged in advance. Are not such protests forms of speech? The relatively minute injury to the owners of property trespassed upon, or to some members of the community whose routine is disrupted, clearly ought to be suffered when balanced against the far greater interests of the entire community in having matters so grave as racial justice, or war and peace, argued effectively and publicly.

When civil disobedience is direct, the protester often argues that the law he breaks is not only bad but invalid—that it violates the Constitution or some other higher legal authority. But the present argument is concerned chiefly with indirect civil disobedience, and Z does not maintain that the trespass (or traffic, etc.) statute is invalid. Nor does he deny the fact that the civil disobedient does technically violate it. He argues simply that, under the circumstances, that violation is outweighed by larger considerations, and hence that such valid but minor rules of order cannot here be properly invoked. He insists that the right to powerful protest, even deliberately disobedient protest, must prevail.

3. THE REPLY

The argument Z presents is an appealing one. All those who are eager to protect and extend the freedom of speech and political debate will naturally be inclined to view it with sympathy. This sympathy will be in many cases reinforced by justifiable confidence in the good character and high purpose of the persons who undertake such indirect civil disobedience. But is the argument sound? I think that it is not; and bad arguments must be rejected, however honorable the cause in which they are presented.

The argument has two grave faults. The first, and more fundamental, concerns the central claim that civil disobedience is a form of speech. Greatly exaggerating the element of truth in this claim, Z's argument seeks support in a chain of Supreme Court decisions that, although important, cannot rightly be applied to cases of indirect civil disobedience. The second fault is more technical, stemming out of the first. It concerns a misconception, embodied in Z's argument, of the role of the courts in these matters and of the function of the balancing process courts must sometimes undertake.

Fault One. Z's argument makes much of Supreme Court decisions in which protesters have been upheld, although their acts appeared to violate existing statutes. But such decisions, though their effects have been to expand the protection of political speech, have been essentially based on one or another of three grounds, no one of which applies to the pure case of indirect civil disobedience.

(a) In some cases these decisions have held that the law violated was itself an unconstitutional restriction of some kind, and because the legislature had exceeded its authority

෨ *Case 17. The United States Supreme Court has ruled that the protest burning of one's draft card is not a form of symbolic speech protected by the First Amendment to the United States Constitution. In doing so, it upheld a 1965 federal law specifically making the deliberate destruction of draft cards a crime. In the case of U.S. v. O'Brien (391 U.S. 367, 1968), Chief Justice Earl Warren, speaking for the Court in a 7 to 1 decision wrote:*

We cannot accept the view that an apparently limitless variety of conduct can be labelled "speech" when the person engaging in the conduct intends thereby to express an idea. However, even on the assumption that the alleged communicative element in O'Brien's conduct is sufficient to bring into play the First Amendment, it does not necessarily follow that the destruction of a registration certificate is constitutionally protected activity. This Court has held that when "speech" and "nonspeech" elements are combined in the same course of conduct, a sufficiently important governmental interest in regulating the nonspeech element can justify incidental limitations on First Amendment freedoms.

O'Brien argued, in effect, that a law specifically prohibiting the destruction of Selective Service registration certificates abridged

in enacting the statute, the deliberate disobedience of it could not, in the last analysis, be held wrong or unlawful. This has been true of decisions in which the law apparently broken was one that, unconstitutionally, required or supported the segregation of the races.

A coordinate category would be that of laws struck down because, whatever their superficial object, their effect is clearly the restriction of speech in violation of the First Amendment. Argument in this vein has long continued regarding statutes penalizing citizens for the defacement or destruction of patriotic or other symbols—flag-desecration statutes, special pun-

his freedom to communicate ideas through such an act. The Court replied: "A law prohibiting the destruction of Selective Service certificates no more abridges free speech on its face than a motor-vehicle law prohibiting the destruction of drivers' licenses, or a tax law prohibiting the destruction of books and records."

Is the constitutional power of Congress to raise and support armies and to make all laws necessary and proper to that end an interest sufficiently important to override those incidental restrictions in this context? The Court held that it is. Chief Justice Warren continued:

We think it clear that a government regulation is sufficiently justified if it is within the constitutional power of the government; if it furthers an important or substantial governmental interest; if the governmental interest is unrelated to the suppression of free expression; if the incidental restriction on alleged First Amendment freedoms is no greater than is essential to the furtherance of that interest. We find the 1965 amendment to the Universal Military Training and Service Act meets all these requirements. ࿓

ishments for the destruction of one's draft card, and the like. The punishment, in such cases, may be imposed although property loss is suffered by no one (save the offender) and no obstruction or inconvenience is inflicted upon the government or its agents. The Supreme Court has thus far held that if such statutes advance some substantial government interest, itself not related to the suppression of speech, and if the consequent limitation of "symbolic speech" is therefore incidental and minimal, the laws in question will not be struck down. (See Case 17.)

A few civil disobedients may well argue that the laws they break are truly unconstitutional in that the suppression of speech they impose is, in fact, not incidental but the real

Case 18. A flag-desecration statute, which makes it a misdemeanor publicly to "mutilate, deface, defile or defy, trample upon, or cast contempt upon either by words or act [the American flag]" is in force in the State of New York, similar to those in force in all other states and the District of Columbia.

Sidney Street, a veteran of World War II and holder of the Bronze Star, upon hearing that James Meredith had been shot in Mississippi during his civil rights march of June 1966, publicly burned a forty-eight-star American flag in New York. "If they let that happen to Meredith, we don't need an American flag," he told the arresting officer.

His conviction under the flag-desecration statute was appealed to the U.S. Supreme Court by attorneys of the American Civil Liberties Union. Their brief in his defense, which appears in their periodical Civil Liberties (December 1967), said, in part:

[Sidney Street had] a right to communicate anger to his fellow citizens in a way that inflicted no injury upon them. The manner by which he chose to express his anger represented his belief that a society that fostered, and a government that tolerated, the conditions which Meredith was himself protesting, betrayed his trust.

purpose and effect of such laws. Were that established, such statutes ought indeed to be quashed. (See Case 18.) But, in any event, such cases are not applicable to the sort of disobedience—disobedience of minor statutes admittedly worthy in themselves—that Z is here concerned to defend.

(b) More pertinent to Z's argument are the cases in which the laws in question were not themselves unconstitutional—as when protesters convicted of trespass in the lower courts have later been exonerated. But the principle upon which such reversals have been based is that in such cases perfectly good laws had been used by local authorities to effect a clearly unconstitutional result. Patent racial discrimination being no longer permitted, some local governments have sought to

For the moment, therefore, he sought to express his belief by destroying what he regarded as the official symbol of trust. . . . The right of government to construct such symbols is not in question. What is in question is the power of government to prevent the people from communicating, by actions relating to a symbol, a contrary message.

This conviction may be affirmed by the Court only if it is ready to decide that the First Amendment right of free expression can be exercised only by the means that those in power choose to permit. . . .

The need for continuing exploration of the expanding application of the First Amendment is as apparent from the headlines as it is from the reported decisions of the state and federal courts. To choke off the peaceful, though non-verbal, means by which our disaffected, discontented and—for many—formerly disenfranchised citizens can make their message known is both unconstitutional and unwise. It runs the risk of reaping the whirlwind. To foreclose the communication of ideas not only deprives persons of the rights guaranteed them by the First Amendment but deprives society of its most effective means for self-correction.　ଈ❧

evade the prohibition and quite deliberately to achieve the same wrongful ends by applying otherwise reasonable statutes concerning disturbance of the peace, or trespass. Subterfuge of this sort cannot be tolerated; hence such convictions have been struck down.

Perhaps the clearest illustration of this principle is provided by a Maryland case in which black students were found guilty of a violation of the state's trespass statute after the manager of a restaurant refused them service specifically because of their race and filed a complaint when they took seats and refused to leave until served. The conviction was reversed by the Supreme Court. In a concurring opinion, Justice Goldberg wrote that the decision of the Maryland court in sustaining the conviction for trespass cannot

be described as "neutral," for the decision is as affirmative in effect as if the State had enacted an unconstitutional law explicitly authorizing racial discrimination in places of public accommodation. A State, obligated under the Fourteenth Amendment to maintain a system of law in which Negroes are not denied protection in their claim to be treated as equal members of the community, may not use its criminal trespass laws to frustrate the constitutionally granted right. . . . [Bell v. Maryland, 84 S. Ct. 1814, 1964.]

(c) Closest of all to the cases Z defends are those in which the Supreme Court has struck down convictions, under wholesome statutes, where the application of these statutes—libel laws, breach of the peace laws, etc.—has not been devious but simply in error. There are some things, the Court has held, (as in The New York Times case mentioned earlier) that even good laws may not prohibit, and though valid on its face, the statute in question may not be applied to the act in question because of the pressing and fundamental need to protect that kind of act under those kinds of circumstances.

Now the case of the indirect civil disobedient—say one who deliberately trespasses to protest the testing of nuclear weapons—is importantly different from all of these three types of earlier decision. That is:

The law broken (say, one of trespass) is not one that is itself unconstitutional or otherwise intrinsically invalid.

The law broken is not one that is being used deviously to accomplish indirectly what would be, if done directly, a violation of the Constitution. The conviction of indirect civil disobedients is not subterfuge; indeed, the enforcing officers often publicly sympathize with the goals of the disobedients but cannot, in their official capacities, fail to respond to the deliberate violation of law.

The analogy with the third type of case is closest, but is still not good enough. The specific act in which the indirect civil disobedient engages—remaining on another's property where he has no legitimate business after being formally requested to leave, or lying in the street specifically in order to block traffic, etc.—whatever its motivation, is not the sort of thing that requires constitutional protection. Political criticism may be protected, even when it appears to violate libel laws, because intrinsically such critical activity is a kind of thing that must be encouraged and defended; lying on the street, or sitting on the floor of an office, are not, intrinsically, acts of that kind.

The legal argument Z presents breaks down, in other words, because of a fault in the premise upon which the whole depends—the claim that indirect civil disobedience is *essentially* a form of speech. Speech may indeed take many forms, and disobedients do generally wish to communicate important ideas. But their wish is one thing, their act another. Whatever they may wish to accomplish through it, their disobedient act has a clear outward form that is indisputable. It is true that human acts do not fall neatly into categories labeled "speech" and "nonspeech" but are often of mixed character, and it is true that context is needed to determine the full significance of an act. But it does not follow from all of this that an act becomes principally and essentially an act of speech simply as a result of the actor's *wish* that it be so regarded. The deliberate violation of a trespass statute (or the like) that is not being deviously employed, whatever the motivation of the violators, cannot reasonably be treated as one of the forms of speech deserving constitutional protection. When the civil disobedient insists that his act—in spite of its specific nature, which is obvious and undeniable—was at bottom speech because of his aims in performing that act, he expands the notion of "speech" so extraordinarily that virtually nothing is left that it may not then be claimed to encompass. Such generalized protection was not the original intention, nor is it the proper present function, of the First Amendment of the American Constitution.

Fault Two. The second major fault in Z's argument lies in his conception of the role of the courts in balancing interests. He argues that the interests protected by the First Amendment (especially its free-speech provisions) are so fundamental that they necessarily outweigh any conflicting interests whatever. So libel laws, or sedition laws, or antilittering laws, and the rest, even if intrinsically worthy, cannot suffice to condemn conduct if that conduct functions as a form of political debate. When the conflicting interests are balanced, the interests of free speech must prevail. Hence Z's conclusion that civilly disobedient acts are constitutionally protected. The mistake here is closely related to the first mistake. It is true that in situations in which the interests of free speech and other community interests need to be weighed against one another by the courts, priority will almost invariably go to the former. What is it in these situations (*The New York Times Co. v. Sullivan* is one illustration) that demands a balancing? It is the unavoidable conflict of certain *kinds* of interests. A community is well served by laws protecting its members from false and libelous defamation, but the community is also served by protecting uninhibited debate. The character and conduct of persons must be protected from vicious attack and yet must often be kept open to attack. Conflict between real community interests arises inevitably; the balancing of "libel" against "the freedom of speech" *must* sometimes be undertaken, or at least contemplated. Normally, and rightly, the courts give by far the greater weight to freedom of speech. Similarly, the reasonable effort to keep the public peace comes naturally into conflict with freedom of speech when a speaker has an inflammatory manner and controversial things to say. In such instances the tensions between the exercise of free speech and the restrictions of otherwise valid laws can be neither avoided nor ignored. Such conflicts oblige the courts to effect some resolution; here again unrestricted debate should and probably will prevail.

Indirect civil disobedience does not arise out of unavoidable conflicts of this kind. The enforcement of reasonable trespass laws (or similar statutes that the disobedient may choose to violate) does not naturally or necessarily collide with First Amendment freedoms. Protecting the safety and convenience of automobile drivers, for example, or the interests of owners of property, normally has nothing whatever to do with the freedom to speak or protest. The courts will balance interests when they must but will rightly refrain from doing so until they must. Z argues that civil disobedience, being intended as a form of political speech, obliges the courts to undertake a balancing process with minor property interests (or interests of convenience) on one side and the freedom to protest on the other. The courts may rightly deny that they have such an obligation. To undertake such a balancing is to admit, in effect, that the defendants, by their deliberate

⊷ঙ্গ   *Case 19. Such a case arose at the Logan Valley Shopping Center, near Altoona, Pennsylvania, when members of a union, picketing a nonunion store in the shopping center, were barred from its parking lot. The lot was privately owned property. But the U.S. Supreme Court held (Food Employees v. Logan Plaza, 391 U.S. 308, 1968) that when, as in the case of this shopping center, an area serves as the community business block, and is not only open to the public but is a focus of public attention, to prevent the entry of picketers would violate the First Amendment guarantee of free expression. In some special circumstances, they said in effect, constitutional rights demand that the public not be barred from private property.*   ঽ≫

choice in violating a trespass or like statute, have the right to select which interests will be balanced against freedom of speech. Prohibiting trespass is a concern about as far removed from free speech as most legal issues can be; yet even these two can come into conflict on rare occasions, whereupon a resolution may then be required. (See Case 19.) But if any deliberate violation of a trespass statute chosen by the protester to be a political act must be balanced against the larger need to protect free speech, then the deliberate violation of any statute, major or minor, if intended as a protest, will have also to be so balanced and may claim the same protection. To accept Z's argument, in short, is to allow a First Amendment defense for any statute violation whatever, if it could reasonably be argued that the violation was intended as some form of protest. This would carry the extension of First Amendment guarantees to the point of absurdity, giving that Amendment as a protective weapon to whomever might wish to stage an illegal protest, whatever its form. A racial bigot protesting civil rights legislation—or any person protesting any laws or policies he happens to think unjust—might then deliberately break the laws he thinks wrongful, or some other unrelated laws, and then go on to argue that his unlawful conduct is protected by the First Amendment. Clearly, that would be pushing the right to protected protest too far. The principle that the Constitution protects against punishment anything claimed to be speech, whether normally so considered or not, is too strong to be adopted in a working democracy.

This is not to say that where the interests of free speech conflict with property or other interests of lesser importance the latter should prevail, but only that unless there is a natural or normal conflict of community interests, such a balancing need not be undertaken.

Three final comments on Z's argument.

First, note that the kinds of conduct that come naturally or normally into conflict with vigorous and open political debate cannot be antecedently clear beyond doubt, or permanently laid down. It is conceivable, for example (but far-fetched), that deliberate peaceful trespass in government offices and buildings could become so common and normal a form of protest that its regular protection as a form of speech would seem less strange than it now does. It may have seemed equally far-fetched, in the early decades of this century, that the interests of picketers should be so circumspectly protected as they now are. But with such developments, our conception of what constitutes a trespass changes, and as the contemplated conduct verges on the legal, it loses all or most of its attraction as a dramatic form of civil disobedience. In short, civil disobedience, especially when indirect, normally requires the selection of an act that is clearly not standard form, and therefore is never likely to be eligible for the protection offered standard forms of protest.

Second, note that a civil disobedient who becomes a defendant in a trespass or similar case may reply to these arguments of principle that they are too general and unspecific to meet his claims: "I do not request a balancing of kinds of interests but of actual interests in one specific situation. I argue not from general principles but only that in this case, under these actual circumstances, the First Amendment protects me." Now this may appear reasonable from his perspective, knowing how genuine was his own effort to publicize a message of community concern. But he could not deny, nor should he wish to if the laws are to be applied even-handedly, that to allow such a balancing in his own case would be to set an important precedent in principle: that an individual, after choosing the form of deliberate disobedience he intends to employ as a form of speech, may seek protection for that disobedient conduct under the Constitution. Any court would find it difficult to allow such a precedent to be set.

Third, and finally, note that the extraordinary expansion of the concept of speech, which Z's argument in effect proposes, is likely, in practice, to have results directly the opposite of those he and most other civil disobedients ultimately seek: it will weaken rather than strengthen constitutional protection of civil liberties. For when one may resort to the First Amendment provision that the freedom of speech is not to be abridged as a defense for virtually any kind of act, the need to qualify the protection it affords will be inescapable. The consequent efforts to define the limits of speech more precisely are likely to produce principles that can later be used to exclude from constitutional protection marginal but effective varieties of speech now safeguarded. As long as "speech" be reasonably construed, the rigor of the First Amendment wording is clear and incontrovertible: "Congress shall make no law" that abridges its freedom. When the concept of speech is unreasonably expanded, the infringements every democrat dreads may enter through the back door, not by "abridging" the freedom of speech but by carefully prescribing what "speech" may encompass. That would be a most unfortunate outcome. But it is the outcome to which Z's argument may lead, were that argument ever accepted by the courts. Happily, its acceptance is quite improbable.

4. SOME STRATEGIC CONSIDERATIONS

There are important strategic reasons, from the protester's own point of view, for not claiming that his deliberate disobedience is protected against punishment by constitutional guarantees. The long-range goal of most disobedients is the achievement of some needed social remedy, brought about by rousing the conscience of the community. To this end, they dramatically exhibit their own deep concern and moral repugnance toward a continuing injustice. Civil disobedience may be reasonably effective in communicating that concern and repugnance, and in prodding others until they share those feelings—providing the depth and sincerity of the disobedients' own commitment is beyond doubt or dispute. Exhibition of that full commitment may bring an apathetic community—or part of it—to begin to reflect upon existing institutions or policies.

Now, as I have argued earlier (see Chapter IV, Section 3), a willingness to accept public punishment for a deliberate public violation strongly reinforces the general credibility of that commitment. But any effort to have the illegal conduct excused *because* it is a protest sharply reduces its effectiveness *as* a protest. If, after having disobeyed the law to make a dramatic self-sacrifice, one then seeks to avoid the penalty that makes it a sacrifice, the depth and completeness of his commitment is very likely to be questioned. Civil disobedience can be a powerful moral gesture; from the viewpoint of one who employs it, one very strong reason for not seeking legal immunity is that such a move is likely to prove self-defeating by reducing the power of the original act.

Z may reply to this strategic argument in two ways. First, he may admit that seeking protection for his conduct can have the unfortunate consequence of raising some doubt about the depth of his own convictions, but he may maintain that that disadvantage is minor and is more than offset by advantages that would accrue from a successful appeal to the constitutional protection of free speech. The effectiveness of civil disobedience, he may argue, stems chiefly from its needling effect upon a complacent citizenry, its capacity to force public attention to focus upon serious moral issues—whatever may come to be thought of the character of the disobedients themselves. The appeal to the free-speech argument has, as one byproduct, a continuation of that needling, a maintenance of public attention upon the moral issue raised. Second, he may argue that the appeal for constitutional protection, if successful, may encourage many other concerned citizens to employ similar tactics where the issues are similarly grave, broadening the effectiveness of moral protest.

These are difficult claims to weigh, because (like so many judgments in this sphere) they are based upon predictions about public reactions, the accuracy of which is virtually impossible to assess. If Z's argument is never successful in the courts (as seems likely), the prediction underlying the second reply can never be tested. And as for what effect the appeal to the courts will have upon the public's attention, it may be that raising the complicated free-speech issues will muddy the waters, obscuring from public understanding the social objectives for which the protest was originally undertaken.

In any case, the wisdom of alternative strategies, where the responses of a large and varied citizenry must be estimated, is surely a matter upon which reasonable men may disagree. Any civil disobedient contemplating resort to Z's argument must weigh not only the theoretical merit of that argument (which is doubtful) but its strategic impact as well. He must be careful not to underestimate the moral force of the self-sacrificial element in disobedient protest and not to underestimate, in consequence, the deleterious effect upon any civil disobedient protest that would result from the attempt to evade the punishment normally meted out to those who knowingly break the law.

CIVIL DISOBEDIENCE AND THE

NUREMBERG JUDGMENTS

1. THE ARGUMENT

A final argument bearing directly on the defense of civil disobedience arises out of the judgments of the International Military Tribunal at Nuremberg. At the close of the Second World War the victorious powers, with the United States in the vanguard, held lengthy and profound inquiries into the wartime conduct of many individuals who had perpetrated, or helped to perpetrate, almost inconceivable atrocities upon innocent, noncombatant victims. As a result of these trials many persons were put to death, and many more were compelled to serve long prison sentences, not simply because they killed in warfare but because they committed acts that no human being ever has the right to commit, no matter what the circumstances. They committed crimes against humanity and against peace.*

---

* In August 1945, the United States, Great Britain, the Soviet Union, and France adopted the *London Agreement and Charter* (subsequently ratified by nineteen other nations) establishing a tribunal and a procedure for the trial and punishment of Nazi war criminals. (U.S. Executive Agreement Ser. No. 472, 1946.) This Charter defined three broad categories of acts as crimes

Now it is sometimes argued that civil disobedience may be justified by invoking the principles developed at these Nuremburg Tribunals. The argument, if at all plausible, is one to which anyone cognizant of the horror of the acts committed by the defendants at Nuremberg must have some sympathy. Yet its bearing upon specific acts of civil disobedience is problematic. Part of the difficulty arises from the fact that this "Nuremberg argument" has never been fully or clearly formulated. Passing reference to the principles of Nuremberg is fairly common, but it is never quite clear whether the argument is a purely moral one or whether it is intended as a technical, legal defense. Of course the line pursued may vary

---

"within the jurisdiction of the tribunal *for which there shall be individual responsibility*" (emphasis added). It is the first of these categories that is particularly relevant to contemporary civil disobedience: "Crimes Against Peace: namely, planning, preparation, initiation, or waging of war of aggression, or a war in violation of international treaties, agreements or assurances, or participation in a common plan or conspiracy for the accomplishment of any of the foregoing." (Article 6a of the Charter.) Under this Charter the Nuremberg trials were held. The principal decisions were handed down on 30 September 1946 (6 FRD 69) and found a number of defendants guilty of crimes against peace.

The President of the United States, addressing the General Assembly of the United Nations on 23 October 1946, reiterated the central theme of those trials: ". . . twenty-three members of the United Nations have bound themselves by the Charter of the Nuremberg Tribunal to the principle that planning, initiating or waging a war of aggression is a crime against humanity for which individuals as well as States shall be tried before the bar of international justice." (U.N. Gen. Ass. Official Records, 1st Sess. 2d pr., 35th Plenary Mtg. 699, 1946.)

The General Assembly of the United Nations, on the basis of a proposal submitted by the United States delegation, unanimously adopted, on 11 December 1946, a resolution in which it: "Affirms the principles of international law recognized by the Charter of the Nuremberg Tribunal and the judgment of the Tribunal." (U.N. Gen. Ass. A/C 6/69.)

These official acts provide the foundation upon which the legal argument of some contemporary civil disobedients is built.

from case to case, but some general observations upon the relationship between the Nuremberg judgments and acts of civil disobedience will help to clarify a range of questions admitted by all sides to be, although of deep importance, still unresolved.

Persons, not governments, were on trial at Nuremberg. Individuals were accused and convicted of committing crimes against international law and against humanity. It is true that many of the laws these persons were convicted of knowingly violating were not codified at the time the acts were perpetrated. In that sense the laws were *ex post facto*, and unjustly applied. But they were the laws of simple human decency, the prosecution argued, known by every man and needing no codification to take effect. And international law, which is codified, clearly "imposes duties and liabilities upon individuals as well as upon states." So the court at Nuremberg declared. War crimes, it continued, are "committed by men, not by abstract entities, and only by punishing individuals who commit such crimes can the provisions of international law be enforced."

The bearing of this principle upon certain kinds of civil disobedience is not hard to see. If an act would be a crime against international law or against humanity, the individual who commits it is responsible for so doing whether or not he is ordered to do so by his government or military superior. If the Nuremberg principle is sound, it will not suffice to argue in defense of such criminal acts: "I only did what I was ordered to do." Some things a man must not do, no matter who orders him to, or with what authority. And if he does do them he will be answerable, on this principle, not only to God or conscience but to courts of international law as well.

On these grounds some persons—notably some Americans during the war in Vietnam—have refused to obey some apparently lawful orders of their government or military superiors. They have said, in effect:

The war is unjust. Atrocities regularly committed by Americans in the course of it are crimes against international law and against humanity. If I do such things I will be personally responsible for them. I am under a compelling duty not to commit such crimes, and will not do so, and therefore must refuse to obey any order to do so. I do not wish to be disloyal to my country. But I have overriding obligations to humanity and to international legal authority, obligations more powerful even than those owed to my national government. I must, therefore openly and deliberately disobey. [See Case 9(a), p. 68.]

What shall we say of this defense? Note first that the disobedience for which the Nuremberg principles are sometimes held a justification is *direct*. It is disobedience of the law, or lawful order, that is itself deemed wrongful. Conceivably, the Nuremberg argument could apply to the young man who refuses induction into military service during an unjust war, or to the soldier who disobeys the order to kill, or to train others to kill, in such a war. It could not apply to those who disobey another law, having no bearing on the war itself, as a way of protesting the nation's foreign policy. More about that shortly. Furthermore, the argument is directed only at wrongs of a specially blatant and atrocious character. It might apply to a law (or order) compliance with which must result in great human misery or pain; it would not apply to a law or order (even if wrongful) the evil consequences of which are humanly tolerable, and even seriously debatable. These considerations significantly restrict the range of cases in which the Nuremberg argument might be invoked.

Note second that, when presented as a purely moral defense, the Nuremberg argument is, in form, essentially no different from the higher-law justifications discussed at length in Chapter V, Section 4. The truth and applicability of the higher principles appealed to remain to be determined. The disobedient can only do his best to exhibit these higher principles and point out their applications, and then he must take the consequences of his defiance. Taken as a moral justification only, the Nuremberg argument may ultimately prove his disobedience right—but it cannot protect him against the legal punishments his government or military superiors are likely to inflict upon him.

It is when the Nuremberg argument is presented as a legal defense of his conduct, claiming technical validity in the courts of the land, that the matter becomes exceedingly sticky.

2. NUREMBERG PRINCIPLES AS A LEGAL DEFENSE OF CIVIL DISOBEDIENCE

Can the judgments of Nuremberg and the pronouncements of that court serve as an adequate legal defense for persons who resort to them as justification for their own deliberate disobedience of some laws, or lawful orders, of their government? There is no clear answer to this question. It does seem clear that it was the intention of the Tribunal that its principles should have legal force not only in the cases then at hand but over the judicial systems of particular nations in all future cases of similar sort. United States Supreme Court Justice Robert Jackson, chief prosecutor at Nuremberg, gave penetrating and persuasive argument in support of the juridical legitimacy of the Tribunal, as well as the international need for its legal authority. In 1945 he said:

We do not accept the paradox that legal responsibility should be the least where power is greatest. . . . With the doctrine of immunity of a head of state usually is coupled another, that orders from an official superior protect one who obeys them. It will be noticed that the combination of these two doctrines means that nobody is responsible. [Cited by Paul Good, "Laying Freedom on the Line," The Nation, March 1967, p. 368.]

And the Tribunal itself concluded: "The very essence [of the principles established here] is that individuals have duties which transcend the national obligation of obedience." Failure to perform these fundamental duties, it held, was punishable by law. It would surely seem, then, that conscientious performance of these fundamental duties—even when this entails disobedience of the national law—should be defensible by law.

The issues raised by the invocation of such a defense for civil disobedience, however, are exceedingly complex. Both generally, with regard to the theoretical soundness of an argument of this type, and specifically, with regard to the war in Vietnam or any particular war to which the Nuremberg principles are applied while hostilities are in progress, there arise questions certain to be argued in American courts for a very long time to come. While the issues cannot be resolved here, some aspects of them can be clarified.

If the Nuremberg judgments ought to have legal authority in the juridical system of any one country, that country is the United States of America. It was we who provided the major impetus for the trials at Nuremberg; it was we who largely financed them, and administered them, and defended them against criticism; it was we who insisted upon the legitimacy of the findings, and upon the execution of the sentences imposed. The Nuremberg trials had, it is true, much general international support, but from no country was that support more vigorous or more tenacious than our own. The United Nations General Assembly adopted the Tribunal Charter as international law—but it did so on a motion by the United States. And Article VI of the United States Constitution makes international laws to which this country is signatory the supreme law of the land. Justice Jackson himself wrote:

If certain acts in violation of treaties are crimes, they are crimes whether the United States does them or whether Germany does them, and we are not prepared to lay down a rule of criminal conduct against others which we would not be willing to have invoked against us. [Ibid., p. 367.]

Perhaps most important of all, the principle to which civil disobedients are likely to appeal—that individuals as well as governments are responsible for the commission of war crimes— is one that had been developed earlier in the United States Supreme Court. That Court (in another connection) had shown that it has applied from its earliest history "the law of war as including that part of the law of nations which prescribes for the conduct of war the status, rights, and duties of . . . nations as well as . . . individuals." (Ex Parte Quirin, 317 U.S. 1, 1942; emphasis added.) This American decision was cited by the International Military Tribunal at Nuremberg as authority for the proposition that individuals as well as states may be held responsible for the commission of international crimes. It would surely seem that unless the Nuremberg judgments are to be wholly discarded, they must somehow have application in American law.

But that application, although on the surface very attractive to many, faces a number of exceedingly severe technical obstacles. Some of these obstacles can be briefly outlined here.

First, the status of the Nuremberg judgments and opinions, as instruments of law, is confused and uncertain. At best we might say that these judgments and opinions are principles somehow to be incorporated into international law, which is itself of uncertain status; at worst they may be only the *dicta* of an illegitimate court. The authority of the Military Tribunal at Nuremberg is itself much doubted in some legal quarters; many jurisprudents reject the opinions of that court out of hand as unauthorized, and having, strictly, no *legal* force. This uncertainty of status may eventually be cleared up, but it renders the Nuremberg principles, at least for the foreseeable future, a weak reed upon which to rest the entire defense of an otherwise criminal act.

Second, the right to protection under Nuremberg principles (assuming that they do have legal authority) supposes that the laws or orders disobeyed did command acts that were illegal and immoral, crimes against international law or humanity. Now the individual civil disobedient may honestly believe that, and may be prepared to defend that conviction with masses of detailed evidence—but within the country whose national conduct he repudiates he is virtually certain never to win his case. American experience during the Vietnam war exhibits this difficulty vividly. Civil disobedients appealing to the Nuremberg principles in refusing participation in that war may be right in claiming that American involvement in that war is criminal, both in substance and manner. Most American courts, however, will not accept, and usually will not even permit the presentation of, argument to that effect. Even if a court were to accept the Nuremberg principles as having, theoretically, legal force in defending some cases of disobedience (an unlikely admission), it is not going to admit that the Nuremberg principles apply to the specific case before that court. In order to do so, it would have to recognize factual circumstances too grievous and upsetting and will always manage to find that recognition not part of its (the court's) proper business. A legal defense that is theoretically feasible (albeit weak) but never practically successful is not much of a defense at all.

Third, it would be exceedingly difficult to make the Nuremberg principles consistently effective within any national legal system—even if they were accorded general support and respect. This is the grave peculiarity of every argument like the one based on the Nuremberg judgments; any court in a national legal system in holding that its nation is acting illegally and immorally attacks thereby the legal and moral foundations of its own authority. Quite different from normal judgments often rendered against the government and in favor of private citizens, a judgment applying the Nuremberg principles calls into question the moral authority of the entire system, and with it, the legitimacy and authority of the deciding court itself. This reflexive character of the judgment being asked for renders it virtually impossible for a national or state court to allow that the Nuremberg argument provides a successful defense in any given case before it. To do so would be to announce, in effect, that the court is governed by a supreme law higher than, and now in conflict with, the law the court is sworn to enforce. As a purely moral matter one might insist that the court does have such obligations to a higher law. But one who believes that must go on to seek ultimate protection under that higher law, and against the state law, in an appropriately higher court—an

international court, perhaps, or the court of heaven. And
these are the courts in which the civil disobedient may find, if
ever, ultimate justification under Nuremberg principles.

These three considerations weigh heavily against the technical merit of a recourse to the Nuremberg judgments in a
legal defense of an act of civil disobedience. But the technical
merit or demerit of the appeal, although possibly of great
practical importance, is not the protester's deepest concern.
He may be convinced that the Nuremberg judgments *do* carry
authority, both moral and legal, and that they *do* justify his
refusal to obey in the case at hand. He is prepared to pursue
the matter as far as his means and the judicial system will
permit.

Regarding the difficulties that arise in making use of the
Nuremberg principles within a national juridical system—specifically in the American system—the disobedient's answer is
straightforward. A method *ought* to be worked out whereby
these principles *can* be upheld within the American courts. If
we have taken these principles seriously enough to apply
them to others, with ensuing capital punishments, and long-
term imprisonments, we are morally obliged to make them
applicable to ourselves. Ours is a legal system (the American
civil disobedient may argue) that is healthy enough and resili-
ent enough to adopt and incorporate new principles governing national conduct, where the moral content of these principles is clear and accepted and the principles themselves are
badly needed to assist in the guidance of our nation's policies
within the community of nations. And American citizens,
they continue, if not saints, are on the whole decent enough
and honest enough to live up to those principles and to hold
themselves answerable before them. To make this internal

application of the Nuremberg judgments possible, a process of legal adjustment may indeed be necessary. If that is true, it is time that process be begun.

Of course the disobedient must recognize that if such principles were in force their effect would be, strictly speaking, not to justify some acts of civil disobedience but to exonerate some acts that, although disobedient on one level of jurisdiction, prove right and wholly lawful on another, higher level. (See Chapter V, Section 2.)

3. THE NUREMBERG PRINCIPLES AND INDIRECT CIVIL DISOBEDIENCE

As a defense of some instances of direct civil disobedience the Nuremberg principles might prove practical one day; as a defense of indirect civil disobedience they can never serve. Even supposing that the Nuremberg judgments had come to have binding authority within a national legal system, they could be rightly applied only under circumstances in which the alternatives of obedience or disobedience forced a citizen to make a difficult moral choice. If obedience to some law (or order) would somehow involve him in a crime against international law or against humanity, or would in some way clearly indicate even approval or acceptance of that criminal conduct, one might plausibly claim that, forced to choose, he is obliged to disobey the state in obedience to an international and moral law of higher authority. Indirect civil disobedience, however, does not arise under circumstances of this kind.

The Nuremberg principles do have, it is true, a wider reach than is commonly believed. One could not deny their ap-

plicability in some case of deliberate disobedience merely because the disobedient in that case had not been specifically
ordered to commit a particular criminal act. Had there been
such an order the Nuremberg argument would certainly seem
applicable—for when German war criminals sought to defend
some of the atrocities they committed during the Second
World War by showing that they had been doing no more
than following their orders, that defense was rejected on the
ground that they had a clear and unavoidable obligation to disobey blatantly immoral orders. But in other cases, where the
wrongful act was obedient, but not the outcome of an explicit
order to behave criminally, the Nuremberg principle was also
held to apply. The judgments of the Tribunal made it very
plain that "the true test . . . is not the existence of the order,
but whether moral choice was in fact possible."

Now indirect disobedients, too, are likely to argue that they
face a moral choice. Suppose they are horrified by their nation's foreign policy, and elect to violate a trespass law in protest. Having, as they believe, an obligation to make their revulsion clear, they choose this limited but dramatic way to
do so. Doing so is indeed their choice, and is morally motivated, but nevertheless the Nuremberg argument cannot defend them. For the key question is whether that moral choice
is forced upon them by the law they disobeyed. Would obedience, rather than disobedience, under the given circumstances, have in any way implied participation in or approval
of the international crimes being perpetrated (as the disobedient believes) by his own government? Clearly, for indirect
disobedience it would not. Obedience to trespass laws, traffic
laws, and the like, indicates neither approval nor disapproval,
tacit or explicit, of a nation's foreign policy or military con-

duct. While a citizen may have an obligation to make his moral position clear, he cannot be said to have an obligation, under Nuremberg principles, to do so by breaking laws that themselves have nothing to do with the moral issues in dispute. Of course a man may *choose* to exhibit his moral revulsion by such deliberate indirect disobedience, and there may be much to say (as I have explained at length in earlier chapters) for and against the ultimate justifiability of such disobedience. But the Nuremberg principles, even if of recognized authority, cannot there apply. By the nature of the case, the circumstances under which indirect civil disobedience takes place do not compel the moral choice between participation and nonparticipation (or approval and disapproval) that Nuremberg principles might conceivably protect. Indirect disobedience almost invariably is practiced in situations carefully selected or created by the protester; he decides upon the law he will break, and how he will break it, as the instrument of his protest. In such situations the Nuremberg principles—quite apart from all other difficulties of their application—could not govern.

Finally, if the disobedience is indirect, the same strategic considerations that speak against the protester's seeking protection from punishment under free-speech defenses (see Chapter IV, Section 3) apply with equal force to Nuremberg defenses. Indirect disobedience derives much of its effectiveness from the manifest dedication and sacrifice of those who practice it. Any effort they make to find a legal shield against the normal consequences of their disobedient act is sure to weaken public confidence in their commitment, and thereby to drain from their protest much of its moral impact.

✥ IX ✥

CONSCIENCE, TACTICS, AND LAW

"Philosophy recovers itself," John Dewey wrote, "when it ceases to be a device for dealing with the problems of philosophers, and becomes a method, cultivated by philosophers, for dealing with the problems of men." Following this implied injunction, we have grappled with issues essentially theoretical yet of immediate—and, for many, grave—practical import. Still, with the philosophical enterprise completed, the hardest questions seem to remain unanswered. "Ought I now, under these known circumstances, commit this act of civil disobedience?" Or: "Knowing well the circumstances under which my neighbor's act of civil disobedience was done, and the worthy objectives he sought to advance, what judgment shall I pass upon his conduct? Upon him?" The subsumption of particular cases under general principles is the substance of the moral life; philosophy, however deep or careful, cannot perform that task for a moral agent.

What philosophy can do is clarify the issues and formulate the principles with which individual acts and events may be more fully understood and rationally appraised. It cannot give particular judgments; it can provide the intellectual framework within which such judgments may be wisely made. The development of that framework has been my object here.

The intelligent application of principles to cases requires an awareness of the many relativities and uncertainties in judgment. In view of the increasing frequency with which judgments about acts of civil disobedience are being called for, it would be well to conclude with a brief backward look at the kinds of relativity and uncertainty most commonly faced in this sphere. This will be clearest, perhaps, if pursued under the several headings distinguished in the subtitle of this book: conscience, tactics, and law.

1. CONSCIENCE

Conscientiousness is one of the defining characteristics of civil disobedience. (See Chapter I, Section 7.) But conscientiousness, clearly, is relative to the individual whose conscience it is that obliges the act. This is not to say, of course, that any act, if performed out of honest regard for conscience, is right. But whether the act be genuinely conscientious, in that sense, is of the utmost importance in making some moral judgments about it. It is essential that one be clear about what it is he is passing judgment upon. The lawfulness of the act is one thing. The objective rightness of the act is another; however difficult to determine, that rightness will depend upon some principles of morality independent of the actor *and*, to some degree, his honest intentions and beliefs at the time of acting. But a third, and equally important matter upon which judgment must also sometimes be given is the moral character of the actor. Wrong acts are often done by good men. And that a man is governed, genuinely and deeply, by the demands of his conscience is one factor (but not the only one) that we properly weigh in judging his goodness. Of course the content of conscientious principles varies greatly; some men, out of conscience, do what many others believe to be atrocious, wicked. Even so, the mere fact that an act is performed out of conscience is surely worthy of consideration. If, in obeying his conscience, another man is obliged to do what we believe—in good conscience—morally wrong, the genuineness of that conflict must give us pause. It may lead us to deeper reflection upon our own principles, and perhaps to the development of greater wisdom by all parties. In this sense the civil disobedient—if he is truly that —may indeed be an honorable man, doing service for us all. Even supposing his act is objectively wrong, he may bring us to a better understanding of our own criteria for rightness; and in spite of the illegality and unjustifiability of his act, the goodness of his character may shine through. It is possible, of course, that his act is not only conscientious but also objectively right.

2. TACTICS

Tactical considerations are central in the evaluation of some categories of civil disobedience—at least in those cases in which the disobedience is indirect and the pattern of justification utilitarian. (See Chapter V, Section 5 and Chapter VI, Section 6.) The many tactical factors to be weighed, and their effects upon the advancement of the end sought, need not be reviewed. Two points made earlier, however, deserve reemphasis. First, any appraisal of a tactic must be made with regard both to its success in attaining (or helping to attain) the objective pursued and to the quality of the end in whose name the tactic is employed. Tactics are instruments; we shall want to evaluate the effectiveness of any given tactic in fulfilling its instrumental functions. But instruments, although never properly divorced from their ends, are employed with differing ends in view. These ends are also subject to judgment. Most often, it is true, persons so moved by conscience as to break the law knowingly and publicly are motivated by worthy ends, humanitarian goals all can share. The resort to civil disobedience as a means is extraordinary, but, after all, so are the problems society sometimes confronts. If one comes to recognize a social injustice of monumental weight and scope, far too long endured, and comes to believe, also, that the normal instruments for its remedy have been consistently ineffective and promise little better in the future, he may then conclude, not irrationally, that some tactics of a specially dramatic and forceful nature must be devised. Civil disobedience may then prove an attractive alternative, perhaps both wise and just. On the other hand, it may be quite otherwise. Sometimes it happens that a tactical move will be intelligently chosen and cleverly executed in pursuit of an objective that is intrinsically unworthy, perhaps itself evil. The judgment of particular acts of civil disobedience necessarily supposes some judgment of the end pursued, but no analysis of civil disobedience as an instrument can provide the tools for the moral appraisal of that end.

Second, means and ends interpenetrate. The quality of the end achieved is much affected by the quality of the means used to achieve it. Civil disobedience, therefore, considered as a tactic, as an instrument, must be expected to affect the result attained. If it is disorderly or irrational it will leave the marks of disorderliness or irrationality on the social fabric it helps to weave. If it is rational, restrained, humane, it may serve—even though it is unlawful—to enhance that fabric. The outcome takes the imprint of the instrument.

3. LAW

Laws provide the skeleton upon which the flesh of social justice hangs. But the kinds of laws are many. There are laws that are human and those that are, perhaps, divine; and of the human there are laws of morality and laws of the polity; and in the polity there are the laws of crime and the civil laws; and among crimes are felonies and misdemeanors; and in both of these categories are acts intrinsically wrongful and acts wrongful only because they are prohibited by law. Conflicts of laws—between levels, between jurisdictions, between spheres—are humanly unavoidable. When, therefore, it is argued whether a civil disobedient really did disobey "the law" or really did obey it, we must try to be clear about the codes to which we refer. What is disobedience in one context may well not be so in another. Wisdom in matters of practical judgment is hardly possible without a keen regard for the context in which the act of alleged disobedience took place.

If law is the skeleton of justice, however, it is not its heart. After the context is known, the laws distinguished, and the levels of authority and conflicts of jurisdiction made clear, the moral task remains—that of determining whether, in that context, given those facts, a given law ought deliberately to be broken. That is what civil disobedience is all about.

INDEX